Roses and Revolutionists

The Story of the Clousden Hill Free Communist and Co-operative Colony 1894–1902

Nigel Todd

Dedicated to
Selina Todd

Roses and Revolutionists

The Story of the Clousden Hill Free Communist and Co-operative Colony 1894–1902

Nigel Todd

Five Leaves Publications

Roses and Revolutionists
by Nigel Todd

Published in 2015 by
Five Leaves Publications,
14a Long Row, Nottingham NG1 2DH
www.fiveleaves.co.uk
www.fiveleavesbookshop.co.uk

Second Edition
ISBN 978-1-910170-17-5

Cover photo:
'A Free Communist Colony in England,
Sketches at Clousden Hill Farm,
Forest Hall, Northumberland.'
The Illustrated London News,
8 January 1898

Design and typesetting
Four Sheets Design and Print Ltd.

Printed in Great Britain

Contents

Preface   7

Chapter 1 — Dreams And Schemes   17

Chapter 2 — 'Itinerant Jewish Glaziers'   36

Chapter 3 — Visitors And Rivals   59

Chapter 4 — Liberty, Fame, Romance   75

Chapter 5 — 'And Thus Set The Sun'   94

Chapter 6 — Endnote   104

Preface

This is the story of a group of people who tried to change the world at the end of the nineteenth century. The route they chose was the creation of a small community set on the banks of the River Tyne. Their chosen instrument was an anarchist market garden. But this was by no means an obscure incident in a provincial backwater. At the time, Tyneside was one of the industrial pivots on which the world turned. Over a third of all new shipping was then built in yards on the Tyne and the nearby River Wear. Vast quantities of coal, mined in the pits of Northumberland and Durham, powered factories, railways, ships and therefore trade across entire continents. More menacingly, the guns and warships that poured out of the armaments factories dominated the seven seas. What happened on Tyneside had global significance.

It was here that the revolution was to begin. There was to be a challenge to the social order encompassing, among economic and other alterations, a commitment to win equal rights for women. Amid the successes and set-backs that were a feature of the experiment, there was no dogmatic political exclusiveness: workers' organisations and parties of varying kinds were welcome allies. Similarly, the narrow boundaries between human beings laid down by nationality were disregarded, and a home offered to political refugees drawn from all over Europe. Not surprisingly, the government called the police to keep an eye on one or two people, and there were brushes with the secret agents of the Victorian state — so clandestine that special permission had to be sought from the Home Office to read the relevant police records. And, like Tyneside, the revolutionary scheme itself aroused international attention.

It has been a difficult tale to track down. Mostly, the actors took the public stage momentarily and then left, leaving little behind in the form of written and visual records. Their story survives only in scattered sources. But although the original version of this book, published in 1986, gathered together numerous surviving components, subsequent research unearthed a few additional insights and material, as well as a cartoon, that have been incorporated into this revised edition. From the new evidence we can more fully understand the pattern of life on a radical, late nineteenth century 'land colony'. The experience of the female participants is made clearer. And so, too, is the place of Clousden Hill in a wider Victorian 'back to the land' movement as well as in the longer continuum of environmental politics now so important in tackling the impacts of climate change — the broad, challenging, disparate movement that Colin Ward, who saw the means of humanising our control over economy and society especially clearly, described as 'a land rights campaign for Britain.'[1]

The wider context deserves a special note for two other reasons. Firstly, it's now possible to see the wider dimensions of the tentative Tolstoyan movement in Victorian and Edwardian England.[2] The Tolstoyans, clustered around John Kenworthy and his Brotherhood Church that spread from South London to the North of England in the 1890s, formed a more significant part of an enthusiasm to reconstruct human relationships along egalitarian and co-operative lines than was assumed in the original version of *Roses and Revolutionists*. Of course, it was all quite small scale. But the Tolstoyans, whose newspaper, *The New Order*, carried detailed reports of their own attempt at organising a land colony near Purleigh in Essex, kept in touch with the Clousden Hill anarchists. Interestingly, the principles of communal organisation, economic problems and the working lives of the Purleigh colonists can today be seen as very similar to those of the Newcastle anarchists, serving either as a warning or an exhilarating challenge to those still considering collective living.[3]

The other advance in our knowledge comes from Margaret Willes' book *The Gardens of the British Working Class,*[4] an inquiry into the history of working class interest in gardening and horticulture. Whilst not an overtly 'political' book, it explores how working with the land (whether on allotments, land colonies, small plots, or window and planting boxes in tenements and 'back-to-back' terraces) became a popular response, especially under the factory system, to the alienation of industrial workers from their own creativity. Growing food to eat was fundamental but it was more than simply instrumental. It was also about taking back control over lives and extending the range of what could be achieved, individually or in association with others, to improve drab immediate surroundings by growing all manner of plants.

The powerful appeal of gardening took many forms, some of which could be very political. Among the further discoveries since the first appearance of *Roses and Revolutionists* was the attempt at Wallsend, within walking distance of Clousden Hill, to create an Owenite-inspired co-operative community complete with its own shops, houses, library and even an elementary school and, inevitably, allotments. This project was at its height over the 1860s–1880s, but several of its key personalities, like Robert Douglass, ex-crane engineman and later the secretary of the Wallsend co-operative society that he helped to set up, were still active in the 1890s. Douglass was a keen gardener, too. The close connections between Clousden Hill and the Co-operative Movement were traced in *Roses,* but the presence of an Owenite legacy in the colonists' vicinity was then entirely unknown.[5]

A final reflection on what has changed over the past three decades is to acknowledge the reinvigoration of the British 'back to the land' inclination, widely defined. Margaret Willes relates several growth points such as the renewed demand for allotments and the emergence of the Incredible Edibles communities as well as interest in permaculture. Transition Towns, reacting against the adverse impacts of carbon based economies, have given birth to localised experiments in food production, supporting urban consumers in challenging the major retailers' gas-guzzling distribution systems and 'air miles' intensive importing practices. Coincidentally, inspired by the Fairtrade Foundation and the Co-operative Movement's supermarkets, shoppers have placed Britain at the top of the international ethical league table for buying Fairtrade products, forcing private supermarket chains to follow suit. As a result, the balance between localism and global social and economic responsibility remains a lively debate. Any step in one direction invariably poses questions that are not always easy to resolve.

Pushing back the boundaries of conventional land use has been undiminished from the 1980s onwards. Organic farming has carved out a larger niche, food co-operatives exemplified by Manchester's Unicorn Grocery have sometimes flourished, ironically local government budget cuts have restored natural ways of utilising green space, and community orchards and Apple Days are springing up almost everywhere. The Clousden Hill colonists would have found our present-day concerns fascinating if bemusing. Yet they wouldn't have had far to go to find heirs to their broad tradition.

A short trip on the Tyne & Wear Metro would take them to the Whitley Bay Station Master's Garden. There they would find a large, flourishing and varied community garden developed and maintained by volunteers. Run on eco-friendly principles, the Garden that used to supply flowers to the stations on the Newcastle to the Coast 'loop' line is becoming a sustainable democratic social enterprise, and a very pleasant place. Travelling in the opposite direction, the remains of the Westgate Workhouse, part of a hideous victim-blaming system for dealing with the poverty familiar to the colonists, still mark part of Newcastle's West End where residents are seeking to transform a set of multi-ethnic neighbourhoods through the locally-generated Greening Wingrove initiative. It was created to deal with the area's appalling litter and fly-tipping problems, fed by astonishing levels of consumer waste. Fairly soon, Greening Wingrove found that it was possible to mobilise people by unlocking 'green energies' — working out ways to help neighbours reduce carbon footprints by lowering their gas and electricity bills; recycling rainwater to curb flood risks; reclaiming a local park bowling green and pavilion for a community garden, social events, adult education and a bicycle repairs hub; as well as 'vertical vegetable' growing up the frontages of tightly packed terraced housing, creating more gardens, planting 1400 trees and a new fruit orchard.

Greening Wingrove won support from the Big Lottery's Communities Living Sustainably programme to test ways of coping with the effects of climate change at very local levels. In this it was assisted by the Workers' Educational Association, Britain's oldest national adult education movement, linking student negotiated learning with action for social change. In the North East, WEA members, tutors and staff had created a 'Green Branch' of voluntary activists that has held several regional conferences on the theme of 'Back to the Land'. These, in turn, morphed into substantial projects on the feasibility of locally organised food systems, as well as community renewable energy options. The whole affair would have appealed to Franz Kapir, principal pioneer of the Clousden Hill colony, and political escapee from the suffocating repression of the Austro-Hungarian Empire. In his spare time, Kapir taught French at the Newcastle Workmen's Educational Club in the early 1890s by inviting his students to translate pamphlets on democratic agriculture written by the anarchist philosopher, Peter Kropotkin.[6]

Piecing together this tantalising story required a good deal of help. I would therefore like to thank at least the following (a few of whom, sadly, have died since 1986): Ray Challinor, Raphael Samuel, Ken Weller, Jean Gleghorn, Paul Salveson, Andy McSmith, Tom Marshall, Gordon

Gaskin, Angus Mckie, Heiner M. Becker (International Institute of Social History, Amsterdam), Charlotte Alston (Northumbria University), and the staffs of the Bodleian Libraries, Oxford, the University of Leeds Library (Special Collections), the National Co-operative Archive, the British Library and the British Newspaper Archive, the Library of Political and Economic Science, the National Archives (Kew), Beamish Museum, the People's History Museum (Manchester), the Newcastle upon Tyne Literary and Philosophical Society, the local studies libraries of Newcastle upon Tyne, Gateshead, Sunderland, Leeds and Manchester, and the Northumberland, Tyne and Wear and Durham County Archives. Gratitude is due to Ruth and Selina for their generous support and patience during the original research and writing stage.

Particular appreciation should be accorded to some heroes of the independent book trade – today's Radical Artisans — who brought *Roses and Revolutionists* to life. Mike Kearney of the Federation of Worker Writers was the first publisher. *Roses and Revolutionists* has been in demand since it appeared almost thirty years ago under Mike's People's Publications imprint. And to Bob Jones whose fabulous Northern Herald bookstall frequently enlivens conferences and book fairs. Bob encouraged me to contact Ross Bradshaw of Five Leaves Publications to see if there was scope for a revival. Thanks, Ross, for giving it a go.

Nigel Todd
NOVEMBER 2015

References

[1] Colin Ward, *Talking Green*, (Nottingham, 2012), p.95.
[2] Charlotte Alston, *Tolstoy and his Disciples: The History of a Radical International Movement,* (London, 2014), and see

also her article 'Tolstoy's Guiding Light' in *History Today,* Vol 60, 10 October 2010.

[3] W.H.G. Armytage, 'J.C. Kenworthy and the Tolstoyan Communities in England', in W. Gareth Jones (ed), *Tolstoi and Britain,* (Oxford/Washington DC, 1995).

[4] Margaret Willes, *The Gardens of the British Working Class,* (New Haven and London, 2014).

[5] Nigel Todd, 'The Wallsend Owenites' in *Forum: Co-operative Education in a New Age?*, Vol 55, No. 2, 2013, pp.279–291.

[6] *Northern Echo,* 7 August 1896.

STATEMENT OF OBJECTS AND PRINCIPLES

FOR THE

Proposed Free Communist and Co=operative Colony.

OBJECTS.

1.—The acquisition of a common and indivisible capital for the establishment of an Agricultural and Industrial Colony.

2.—The mutual assurance of its members against the evils of poverty, sickness, infirmity, and old age.

3.—The attainment of a greater share of the comforts of life than the working classes now possess.

4.—The mental and moral improvement of all its members.

5.—The education of the children.

6.—To promote or help any organisation to organise similar Colonies.

7.—To demonstrate the superiority of Free Communist Association as against the Competitive Production of to-day.

8.—To demonstrate the productivity of land under intensive culture.

STATEMENTS OF PRINCIPLES.

MEMBERSHIP—

1.—For the attainment of the foregoing objects, the persons who have signed these principles agree to associate together, and admit, according to vacancies, any one willing to put his Communist principles into practice as a member.

WITHDRAWALS—

2.—Any Member wishing to withdraw, to have full liberty to do so at any time.

ADMINISTRATION—

3.—The business of the Society to be regulated by a Joint Committee of all the adult male and female members, who shall meet every night if necessary to discuss, regulate, and distribute the work among themselves, and settle any other business for the next day, or any future time. All fundamental points to be discussed until unanimity is established.

OFFICIALS—

4.—The Officials of the Society to consist of a Secretary and Treasurer, appointed by the Joint Committee of all the members.

SECRETARY'S DUTIES—

5.—To transact the whole of the Society's correspondence, to keep the accounts, and to enter regularly on the minute book the whole of the transactions of the Society.

TREASURER'S DUTIES—

6—To transact the whole financial business of the Society, according to the agreement of its members.

ACCOUNT BOOKS—

7.—The books and accounts of the Society to be open for the inspection of all its members, or any one interested in the Society.

AGREEMENT—

8.—This Association being constituted on the principles of Liberty and Equality, we do not recognise any other authority but the one of Reason, and no member or members shall have any other power but that of Reasoning.

SOLIDARITY—

9.—We agree that whatever talents we may individually possess, whether agricultural, industrial, or scientific, shall be directed to the benefit of all, by their immediate exercise in all necessary occupations ; also by communicating knowledge to each other, particularly to the young.

HARMONY—

10.—That we each observe the utmost kindness and respect to those who differ from us in opinions.

ARBITRATION—

11.—That should any of the members have a dispute with any other person, we think it advisable to abide by the decision of any person or persons agreed to, to whom the matter in question may have been referred.

PRODUCTION AND DISTRIBUTION.

PRODUCTION—

12.—The work, whether agricultural, gardening, or industrial, to be done on the most advanced principles of scientific research and instruction ; machinery to be used wherever possible so soon as the funds of the Society permit such to be done.

TIME AT WORK—

13.—Except in cases of general agreement, no working time shall be fixed or limited, as we believe that, considering these new conditions, each one will do his best, and work according to his abilities, physically or otherwise.

SUPPLY OF NECESSARIES—

14.—All the members to be supplied with reasonable housing accommodation, with due regard for privacy and families.

ARTICLES OF FOOD—

15.—All articles of food to be supplied to the members, either in the raw state from the common store, or cooked from the common kitchen, free, according to the needs of each ; limitation to take place only in those articles which cannot be supplied in sufficient quantities to all, sick persons, children, and women to have precedence. After they have been supplied, the rest to be distributed according to agreement amongst the remaining members.

CLOTHING AND GENERAL WANTS—

16.—All articles of clothing, etc., to be manufactured as far as possible by the members, and supplied free to all from the general fund ; necessity to regulate the supply.

PARTICULAR WANTS—

17.—For any article where the desire for such is only particular and not general, a small sum previously agreed to shall be handed over to each member weekly or monthly, as arranged, to dispose of according to his or her inclination.

DISPOSAL OF SURPLUS PRODUCTION—

18.—The whole of the surplus production to be sold directly to the consumers at a reasonable price, or exchanged for other useful articles of comfort.

IMPROVEMENTS—

19.—The surplus, after defraying all expenses of the Colony, to be invested in improvements and further extensions. If such is impossible, new Colonies to be started on the same conditions and principles.

DOMESTIC ECONOMY—

20.—All housework, such as cooking, cleaning, washing, etc., to be done on the most improved system, to relieve the women from the long and tiresome work which unduly falls as their share to-day, so as to give them opportunity for leisure and the free exercise of all their faculties.

EDUCATION—

21.—The education of the children to be performed by competent persons, with due regard to their physical as well as mental training.

ALTERATION OR IMPROVEMENT OF THE STATEMENT OF PRINCIPLES—

22.—Any alteration or improvement in this statement of principles can only be done by the unanimous consent of the members.

☞ For many of the above clauses we are indebted to the late eminent Sociologist, E. T. Craig, many of which were applied in connection with his successful Co-operative Colony at Ralahine, county Clare, Ireland.

Since the first issue of this Prospectus, we have leased the Clousden Hill Farm, Forest Hall, near Newcastle-upon-Tyne, for the realization of the above objects.

Chapter One
Dreams and Schemes

Franz Kapir was a man with visionary ideas as exotic as his own nineteenth-century background. Born around 1862 at Schlan, near Prague, a Bohemian region then entangled in the Hapsburgs' Austro-Hungarian Empire straddling central Europe, he was later forced to leave his working-class parents and wander through country after country. Not content with simply following a trade as a tailor of women's clothes, Kapir had educated himself in political philosophy, discovering that the price of holding 'advanced' opinions was official persecution. But extensive travel also perfected his fluency in five languages. It must have helped, too, that this 'vigorous, intellectual and likeable' character[1] was able to 'favourably impress everyone... by his earnestness and unvarying good humour, to say nothing of his experience and erudition.'[2]

What kept Kapir on the move was the fact that he had been an anarchist since 1882. Initially attracted to anarchist direct action in the stifling confines of the Hapsburg Empire, he later became an anarchist-communist seeking the revolutionary transformation of society by peaceful means: 'I was at one time as much a believer in violence as anyone; I now see that violence is no remedy.' Anarchist-communism, personified by Peter Kropotkin and Emma Goldman, dedicated opponents of the Russian Tsarist and other state tyrannies, could claim a wide following in the 1880s and 1890s. Advocating a class struggle for workers' rights and a society where private ownership of agriculture and industry would be replaced by small self-governing communes distributing wealth to people according to their needs, the anarchist-communists spread their agitation across Europe and

North and South America. Sceptical of attempts to win power by parliamentary means, they campaigned for the direct take-over of towns and workplaces by mass action, emulating the Paris Commune of 1871.[3]

Around 1889 Kapir's travels took him to London, then a fairly safe haven for political exiles. Once there, he joined anarchist groups and helped to found the Autonomie Club that brought together international anarchists of various persuasions, meeting in 'a cellar in Windmill Street, off Tottenham Court Road.' The Club, numbering police spies among its members, was closed down by the government in 1894 following a bomb outrage. Kapir, lacking work, had already moved to Newcastle upon Tyne sometime during 1890, earning a living as a ladies' tailor, not very happily as he thought he was asked to work 'almost to deform women instead of helping them.' Once in Newcastle he joined with other tailors as well as students and factory workers to form an anarchist group called the Newcastle Workmen's Educational Club (an adult education format devised by anarchists in Britain). Anglicising his name to Frank Kapper, he contributed to the work of the Club, firstly, by teaching French to 'the English comrades.' His French class was apparently popular and was certainly different: language teachers usually relied on French literary classics as teaching materials, whereas Kapper translated from Kropotkin's books and pamphlets on anarchism and agriculture.[4]

The anarchist club took part in a vibrant agitation on Tyneside and Wearside in 1893-1894, holding open-air meetings on Sundays with Kapper as the main speaker.[5] Early in 1894, the Newcastle anarchists upset the more staid labour leaders locally by calling on unemployed workers to raid food shops to feed their hungry children. Beyond Newcastle, there were reports that anarchist-oriented journals — *Liberty, Freedom,* and *Commonweal* — were circulating in colliery villages, with meetings taking place at Sunderland, Silksworth and elsewhere.[6] A shortage of speakers hindered progress, but by the middle of 1895 *Freedom* could record 'adherents in several industrial centres on the Tyne' and meetings at Sunderland, South Shields, Newcastle, Stanley and Gateshead.[7]

Many anarchists at this time were interested in the impact of science on agriculture, and the consequent possibilities for producing food in abundance. It was a fascination stimulated by Kropotkin, then writing and lecturing on how new technical developments in horticulture might be harnessed to underpin a society based upon self-governing village and town communes. Beginning with articles in the magazine *Nineteenth Century* in 1888, and subsequently with a book entitled *The Conquest of Bread* published (in French) in 1892, Kropotkin proposed applying artificial heating systems, greenhouses (or 'glass culture') and new fertilisers to land cultivation. *Freedom* serialised an English translation of *The Conquest of Bread* in 1893-1894, and anarchists in the North East of England were keen to get hold of copies of the book.[8]

Simultaneously, the question of reorganising agriculture within a democratic framework was raised in the Co-operative Movement. In May 1894, the annual 'parliament' of the retail and producer co-operatives — the Co-operative Congress — met at Sunderland, and on the agenda was a paper dealing with 'Co-operative Agriculture'. It roused the attention of anarchist-communists who tended to have a soft spot for the co-operatives, seeing them as in essence voluntary, open associations of consumers and producers, successfully eliminating the private profit motive but hamstrung by bureaucratic leaderships. *Freedom* urged its readers occasionally to conduct 'a broad Anarchist propaganda... among co-operators.'[9] The opening of the Sunderland Congress was also noteworthy in the North East, prompting special supplements in the local press. Co-ops, after all, were already important enterprises with annual sales of over £2 millions, and large numbers of shops, warehousing, milling and wholesaling activities along the Tyne and the Wear.

Frank Kapper went to Sunderland to look at an exhibition of goods produced in co-operative factories. Intrigued by what he saw, he talked with Congress delegates and got himself a visitor's ticket so that he could listen to the debates.[10] One morning was allocated to the paper on 'Co-operative Agriculture' presented by William Campbell, a Leeds co-operator and veteran advocate of agricultural co-operatives. Neatly linking with the sort of ideas put forward by Kropotkin on the relationship between technology and agriculture, Campbell urged the Co-operative Movement to encourage co-operatives in horticulture. He drew support from a London delegate, the Tolstoyan John C. Kenworthy, who had a knowledge of the American anarchist movement and who 'preached nothing less than Communist Anarchism.'[11] Kenworthy urged the Congress to endorse 'voluntary co-operation on the land' as distinct from the retail co-operative societies opening and managing farms in much the same way as they ran their branch shops.[12] It was a theme that he developed at a

Sunderland Co-operative Society's Central Premises, 1894
PHOTO: NATIONAL CO-OPERATIVE ARCHIVE

Congress 'fringe' meeting held by the Sunderland branch of the Independent Labour Party,[13] and it was here that Kapper met another social visionary named William Key.[14]

William Key was older than Kapper and had a very different life-story. Key had been born into a financially well-off family[15] yet had decided to work at a variety of working-class jobs in his youth. A sailor for twelve years, a pitman for eight years, Key had sold insurance on a part-time basis combined with working as a publican at Sunderland's American Hotel for a further twelve years. He then turned to supplying the army and the navy with flour, beef and clothing from Tavistock House on Sunderland's Borough Road.[16] Through military contracting, Key increased his family's fortune 'ten-fold' and became well known at the War Office and the Admiralty.[17] His real passion was social reform rather than business. From the time he moved to Sunderland's East End in about 1875 he 'identified with almost every movement that had for its object the elevation of humanity in general.'[18] His generosity was said to be 'proverbial', often lending money to workers' organisations at times of crisis, expecting neither interest on the loans nor, probably, any repayment. A socialist rather than an anarchist, Key's socialism was receptive to principles that motivated the anarchist-communists, removing any ideological barriers to collaborating with Kapper.[19]

Both Kapper and Key were excited by the prospect of using modern methods of horticulture to sustain co-operative life-styles. Pooling their ideas, and Key's money, they drew up a plan to found a community, or 'colony', serving as a test-bed for a completely new way of life. When they set about preparing publicity brochures, recruitment of sympathisers and raising funds for the colony they wrote to Kropotkin, asking if he would act as treasurer (or principal fund-raiser). But William Key soon found himself taking on the role when Kropotkin replied: 'I am the least appropriate person, as I was never able to keep accounts of my own earnings and spendings.'[20] Key also used his contacts with Sunderland's trade unions and the ILP to find Kapper a place to stay. This turned out to be at 8 Randolph Street, only a short distance from Tavistock House, and then occupied by two other tailors. It was a very 'political' house. One of the tailors, R.D. Craig, was president of the Sunderland Trades Council, vice-president of the local ILP and had been elected only recently as an ILP Councillor for the town's Bridge Ward. From Randolph Street, Kapper brought together 'about 20' people 'willing to join the colony' from Sunderland and other parts of Wearside and Tyneside.[21]

Recruits could have been relatively easy to find both among the anarchists and within the ILP's idealistic ranks. Many ILPers saw socialism as a reformation of everyday human relationships: love, equality and fraternity were powerful impulses within the Party in its early years. And if the ILP's politics revolved around limited programmes of reform, not a few rank-and-file members retained a suspicion of 'authority' that meshed with the anarchist-communists' hostility towards anything that gave a few people power over others. The Sunderland branch of the ILP was identified with this stream of 'libertarian' socialism. Their choice of Kenworthy to address a public meeting during the Co-operative Congress was one indicator, and another was an (unsuccessful) invitation to William Morris to become their parliamentary candidate early in 1894.[22] The Sunderland ILP was extremely active throughout 1894–1895, reflecting the Party's country-wide expansion. Branches had opened in central Sunderland, in the town's East End, and at nearby Monkwearmouth. A Labour Club and 'literature depot' were located in the High Street, regular open-air public meetings were organised and a small group of ILP and trade union Councillors had been elected to Sunderland Borough Council. A Council election, however, produced an unexpected, and unwelcome, problem.

In March 1895, Kapper and Key issued a prospectus addressed 'To all Friends and Sympathisers of Land Colonisation', and especially to the 'more fortunate brothers and sisters' with jobs and therefore money to help launch 'a Free Communist and Co-operative Colony', the name reflecting the dual genesis of the idea. The prospectus promised that eventually 'all sums advanced will be returned.'[23] This statement of intent was reported in the Sunderland press, provoking a sceptical but not entirely dismissive reception from the Liberal *Sunderland Daily Echo*. By contrast, the Tory *Sunderland Herald & Daily Post* was driven to strident outrage and ridicule. For several days in March the *Post* sniped at the colony scheme and its promoters, singling out William Key as a man who 'during the last 20 years we have met... as the representative of so many fads and interests.'[24] Kapper leapt to his new friend's defence, condemning the paper's 'unpleasant personal remarks.'[25]

The *Post's* attacks might have died away but for a sudden decision by the ILP to nominate Key as their candidate for the by-election in Sunderland's East Ward in April. Alarm bells rang at the *Post* because there were two rival Tory candidates standing in the by-election and no Liberal: it looked as though Key might actually win with the help of a split Tory vote. The *Post* set off to save the day by convincing Tory voters to unite behind one candidate to keep the socialist out. The paper unleashed a fierce onslaught on Key: 'a well-known believer in Spiritualism and Socialism and other impossible schemes, the latest of which... is the proposal to borrow money to commence a Socialistic or Communistic community in the neighbourhood of Sunderland.'[26] Next day the *Post* openly denigrated Key: 'the late host of the American Hotel [is] not a fit or proper person to send as [a] representative to the Council. The Socialist candidate may be a very clever man but he is full of impossible schemes' such as the communist colony.[27] Virulent criticisms continued with the colony pushed well to the fore as an example of the terrifying evils of socialism. Key was described as either 'a genius before his time, or only a man with a hive of Socialistic bees in his bonnet'[28]and again: 'We pity the community if ever it has to be governed by the Communistic Co-operative Colony or the Labour agitator class.'[29] Key was quite capable of hitting back. At public meetings he stood his ground as 'a Collectivist out-and-out', receiving rounds of applause whenever he denounced the editor of the *Post* (who was generally listening in the audience).[30] But Key could not stop the 'red scare', as the Tory voters united successfully behind one of their candidates.

The plan for a 'Free Communist and Co-operative Colony' evolving at Sunderland in 1894–1895 would have found echoes elsewhere. A great many land colonies, by no means all anarchist, were formed during the last decade of the nineteenth-century in England and the Americas. There was a lengthy history of communist communities in North America whose experience was made known in Britain by books such as Charles Nordhoff's *Communistic Societies of the United States* (London, 1875), and popularised by Arthur Baker in a series of articles for the Sunday newspaper, the *Weekly Times and Echo*, that had a sizeable circulation in labour and socialist circles.[31] Towards the close of the century, communist colonies sprang up in 'frontier' regions, principally in the North Western United States[32] and in Central and South America. There was curiosity in the progress of the South American ventures with frequent press reports featuring Colonia Cosme in Paraguay (formed by Australians but which sought members in Britain), Los Buenos Amigos in Peru and Topolobambo in Mexico.[33]

A handful of the better-known, if generally short-lived, colonies are now relatively well-documented.[34] The

Labour Colony established at Starnthwaite, near Kendal, in 1892, for example, included two of the ILP's most popular propagandists, Enid Stacey and Katherine St. John Conway (who acted as secretary), and Dan Irving who became prominent in the Marxist Social-Democratic Federation. Starnthwaite floundered in evictions and confusion in 1893 when the members clashed with the autocratic traits of the colony's chief financier, but the aims and practices of the colonists generated interest.[35] The Tolstoyans' colony at Purleigh in Essex was reported in great detail in *The New Order* with first-hand accounts of the horticultural work, the colonists' domestic lives and their efforts to cultivate an appreciation of their aims. Purleigh eventually experienced internal tensions and closed in 1904. More enduring was the Whiteway Colony, near Stroud in Gloucestershire, that emerged in 1898 by a roundabout route from Purleigh and Croydon's Brotherhood Church (where first Kenworthy and then Arthur Baker were employed). After a period of immense hardship for the colonists at Whiteway as they tried to insist on a free communist life-style without money, local suspicion and unwelcome Home Office interference, the colony survived, and still exists as a form of co-operative community.[36]

Charting the way to a new society through self-contained communities was not unique, and within living memory working-class movements had taken up land settlement schemes during the period of 'Owenite' Co-operation (the 1820s–1840s). Co-operative communities at Orbiston, Exeter, Ralahine, Assington, Cork, Dublin, New Harmony and Birkacre[37] went for economic self-sufficiency as far as possible. But they tried to demonstrate by their social relations and educational activity that it was feasible to create a 'New Moral World' rooted in harmony and a communal life-style. Chartism, too, flirted with land schemes in the 1840s, although favouring smallholdings based on 'model villages'.[38] Neither the Owenites nor the Chartists succeeded on their own terms, but, arguably, their failures could always be attributed to surmountable deficiencies in management and financing rather than to fundamental flaws in the ideas behind them, or to alleged shortcomings in 'human nature'.

So, the community dream exercised a recurring appeal. The tenacity of communitarianism could be found in the land nationalisation campaigns of the 1890s when the Durham and Northumberland miners, looking back to Owenite Co-operation, adopted a manifesto that included: 'the great ideal of living in perfect harmony in co-operative communities, each seeking the good of all and all seeking the good of each, broadly based upon the land.'[39] And in the Northumberland pit villages during this period there was an awareness of the commune-based form of socialist society idealised by William Morris.[40]

That Owenite ideas were still circulating during the latter part of the nineteenth-century was due in no small measure to co-operators and sociologists such as E.T. Craig who had been associated with the community at Ralahine summarised in his book *The Irish Land and Labour Question, Illustrated in the History of Ralahine and Co-operative Farming*, published in 1882. Extracts from Craig's book were reprinted in C.W. Stubbs' *The Land and the Labourers: Facts and Experiments in Cottage Farming and Co-operative Agriculture*, issued in 1891 as part of a wave of books focussed on land colonisation. Craig retained respect among the more radical land reformers with whom he associated until his death at the age of ninety in 1894. His last newspaper article, entitled 'Why I am a Socialist and a Co-operator in Production', was written for the anarchist magazine *Liberty* only days before his death, and the editor had no hesitation in claiming, apparently with the support of Craig's son, that Craig sympathised with anarchist-communism.[41]

Frank Kapper and his collaborators at Sunderland had also 'read of the experiments made at Queenwood by Robert Owen and at Ralahine by E.T. Craig', and Craig's influence was readily acknowledged. Kapper reportedly confirmed that Craig's book 'practically decided his action.'[42] In fact, the first six out of eight objectives listed in the prospectus distributed by Key and Kapper in March 1895 would not have looked out of place in an Owenite manifesto:

1. The acquisition of a common and indivisible capital for the establishment of an Agricultural Colony.

2. The mutual assurance of its members against the evils of poverty, sickness, infirmity, and old age.

3. The attainment of a greater share of the comforts of life than the working classes now possess.

4. The mental and moral improvement of all its members.

5. The education of the children.

6. To promote or help any organisation to organise similar colonies.[43]

The difference was that Kapper and Key were not simply repeating notions of 'alternative communities' devised by earlier generations. They connected politically, if uneasily, with the movement for land reform in their own times. The 'Land Question' was a burning obsession of late-Victorian politics. Fired by injustices flowing from the inequitable ownership of agricultural land, it spoke to claims of mass unemployment allegedly caused by large numbers of people migrating to the cities from rural areas. 'Back to the land' was a slogan common alike to radical reformers, looking to undermine the power of the Tory landed class, and to paternalistic members of the aristocracy worried about crime and unrest in the over-crowded slums.

An array of organisations and individuals flourished in this milieu, ardently promoting their own prescriptions. One cross-section of the mixed spectrum was revealed at a conference on 'Land, Co-operation and the Unemployed' held at London's Holborn Town Hall in October 1894, an event described by socialists as 'perhaps a little more charitable than principled.'[44] The motives of the land colonisers present at the conference ranged from returning to a supposedly idyllic ruralism; the conversion of labourers into respectable property-holders; the transfer of the urban unemployed from workhouses to farm colonies where they could be trained in agricultural skills and then sent to Canada and New Zealand; and the advocacy of agricultural co-operatives.

Divisions of opinion could be sharp. The more conservative commentators on rural affairs perceived real dangers in the activities of the land reformers. Russell M. Garnier, who wrote monumentally on land issues, rounded on the radical land colonisers — especially 'the English Land Colonisation Society, the Home Colonisation Society... plans for... co-operative tenancy... the Labour Colony at Starnthwaite' — accusing them of importing the class struggle into the countryside: 'The nationalisers of the land, having always concentrated their attention on realty, are able to furnish the Socialists and Anarchists with their best weapons for attacking this out of the many forms of property which they seek to annihilate. The individual who sets up a plough is to have the same freedom over the soil as the individual who sets up a windmill over the air. He may claim identical powers of sale, gift, and transfer over the produce of land as the fisherman can claim over that of the ocean. But he may no more appropriate the soil into which he drives his share than the fisherman the salt water into which he plunges his net.'[45] Garnier undoubtedly over-reacted against land reformers, many of whom shared his objective of incorporating the 'labouring classes' into the Victorian social order. But he did accurately detect the unmistakable signs of an anarchist-communist 'infiltration' into the land colonisation movement.

Among those present at the Holborn conference was John C. Kenworthy, this time as secretary to the English Land Colonisation Society. Kenworthy's interventions confirmed attempts to convert elements of the land reform movement to anarchist (or Tolstoyan) perspectives. He reported that a struggle within the English Land Colonisation Society had already resulted in a decision to adopt 'co-operative or communal tenure... and co-operative cultivation... [as] the possible beginning of an entire alteration in our economic system.' This 'entire alteration' would be rooted in co-operative small-holdings linked with city co-operative stores. As a first step a 'colony of small-holders, now projected at Horeham Road, Sussex' would be brought 'into relation with a co-operative centre, now in the course of formation at Croydon.'[46]

In the midst of the struggle over the 'land question', Kapper and Key took their cue from Kropotkin, who was respected by at least a segment of the land reform movement. The Sunderland prospectus for the Free Communist Colony drew heavily on a restatement of Kropotkin's findings in a study of intensive horticulture on the island of Guernsey, and was sent to journals such as the *Horticultural Review* read by farmers and by other people interested in the future of the land.[47] At the same time, it was made known in the North East of England that the group brought together by Frank Kapper wished to: 'acquire a piece of land, and cultivate it intensively, growing vegetables at first... and to organise a dairy and poultry farm as a source of immediate income... it is intended... to put a large proportion of the land under glass, and thus to endeavour to realise Prince Kropotkin's prediction that vineries will grow up around the pits of Northumberland and Durham, where artificial heat from coals can be easily obtained at low prices.'[48]

Reflecting anarchist-communist beliefs, the prospectus included two of Kropotkin's ideas in the list of objectives:

7. To demonstrate the superiority of Free Communist Association as against the Competitive Production of today.

8. To demonstrate the productivity of land under intensive culture.[49]

THE PROJECTED FREE CO-OPERATIVE COLONY.

AN APPEAL TO ALL FRIENDS AND SYMPATHISERS OF LAND COLONISATION.

Never in the whole history of humanity has the need for practical action been so pressing as it is to-day. Our cities and towns are overcrowded, the unemployed workers can be numbered nearly by millions, industry is almost at a standstill, and starvation, misery, and vice are in the homes of the people. Shall we remain inactive in face of all this? No, the question, "What's to be done?" needs a reply, and our answer is: "Get the workers back to the land to cultivate the soil; but not on the lines of the average English farmer and his labourers, but on principles as explained by practical scientists, and already adopted by some practical men."

The *Review of Reviews*, in its notice on a valuable paper of Prince Krapotkin's, says:—"Prince Krapotkin's chief illustrations, however, as to the possibility of intensive agriculture are taken from the Channel Islands, and notably from Guernsey. Guernsey has 1,300 persons to the square mile, and has more unproductive soil than Jersey; but Guernsey leads the way in the matter of advanced agriculture, because Guernsey is being practically roofed in. The Guernsey kitchen garden is all under glass. Prince Krapotkin found in one place three-fourths of an acre covered with glass; in another, in Jersey, he found vineries under glass covering 13 acres, and yielding more money return than that which can be taken from an ordinary English farm of 1,300 acres. Each acre of greenhouse employs three men. The cost of erecting them is about 10s. per square yard, excluding the cost of heating pipes. The 13 acres are warmed by consuming a thousand cart loads of coke and coal. Prince Krapotkin sees that before long immense vineries will grow up round the coal pits of Northumberland, where artificial heat can be obtained from coals selling at the rate of 3s. per ton."

Similar examples can be given, but the above will suffice to explain our intentions, which are as follows:—

1. To buy or rent on long lease sufficient land to enable us to organise an industrial colony.

2. The whole of the land to be cultivated intensively, either as vegetable gardens or orchards.

3. A portion of the land to be covered with glass immediately, and extended as funds permit.

4. By the above method of cultivation, and by attention to articles of consumption hitherto almost entirely supplied by the Channel Islands and Continental countries, to demonstrate that the land can be worked with benefit, even under the present conditions.

5. To give an object lesson to those who are really desirous of solving the unemployed problem. If, as Krapotkin points out, a large number of workers were settled prosperously upon the land, it would not only give them employment, but by their increased purchasing power of manufactured articles, would give an impetus to such industries, thus providing employment for a still greater number.

6. To organise a poultry and dairy farm as a source of immediate income.

7. To introduce as many industries into the Colony as possible.

8. To invest all surplus funds in extensions, or in the establishing of other Colonies.

9. To accept anyone as a member, according to the statement of principles.

10. The Colony to be organised on the principles of Co-operation and Free Communism.

These brief statements embody the principles on which it is proposed to erect the structure. To develop these ideas, sympathy and material assistance are necessary, and as the only capital possessed by the workers at the present time is their labour force and the will to work, we venture to appeal to all our more fortunate brothers and sisters to take the foregoing proposals into consideration, and to aid us as far as they are able in the work in which we are engaged. All sums advanced will be returned as the Colony progresses. Should any further information be desired, the Secretary will be happy to supply same. Hon. Treasurer, William Key, Tavistock House, Sunderland. Hon. Secretary, F. Kapper, 8 Randolph-street, Sunderland.

Horticultural
Review
April 1895

Kapper and Key intended to 'give an object lesson to those who are really desirous of solving the unemployment problem. If, as Kropotkin points out, a large number of workers were settled prosperously upon the land, it would not only give them employment, but by their increased purchasing power of manufactured articles, would give an impetus to such industries, thus providing employment to a still greater number.'[50] These perspectives probably set the project apart from much of the rural mythology of the 'back to the land' movement. Kapper accepted the continued existence and value of manufacturing industry, and with Kropotkin he saw the role of land colonies as one of pointing towards the integration of industry and agriculture. Distinctively, the Sunderland colony would rest on the application of 'new technology'. The world to be built on the banks of the Tyne and Wear by Frank Kapper and his comrades would be a step forward into a future of technology, industry and agriculture fused by communal organisation into a new society guaranteeing freedom from poverty.

References

[1] *Le Temps,* 29 September 1897; *Northern Echo,* 7 August 1896.

[2] *Newcastle Daily Chronicle,* 16 November 1897.

[3] Peter Kropotkin (1842–1921) was a Russian Prince who rejected Tsarist rule and combined in anarchism, science, exploration and adventure, as well as spells as a political prisoner. He spent over thirty years exiled in Britain after 1886, becoming the leading exponent of anarchist-communism. See: P. Kropotkin, *Memoirs of a Revolutionist,* (New York, 1899), and James W. Hulse, *Revolutionists in London: A Study of Five Unorthodox Socialists,* (Oxford, 1970); Paul Avrich, *Anarchist Portraits,* (Princeton, 1988)

Emma Goldman (1869–1940) was also born in Russia and campaigned through the 1890s in the United States championing free speech, fighting for women's rights and battling against arrest and police harassment and sweatshop working conditions. She was one of the best known anarchist speakers of her time. See: Emma Goldman, *Living My Life,* (New York, 1970 edn.), 2 vols; Paul Avrich and Karen Avrich, *Sasha and Emma: The Anarchist Odyssey of Alexander Berkman and Emma Goldman*, (Cambridge, Mass., 2012).

For Kapir's background see: *Northern Echo,* 7 and 11 August 1896.

[4]   *Le Temps, op.cit. Northern Echo, op.cit.* H.W. Nevinson, *Changes and Chances*, (London, 1923), p.123.

[5]   *Le Temps, op.cit.*

[6]   *Freedom*, April 1894.

[7]   *Ibid.,* June 1895.

[8]   *Liberty*, April 1894; Peter Kropotkin's, *The Conquest of Bread,* was republished by Penguin Classics in 2015 and there is an informative review by David Priestland in *The Guardian,* 4 July 2015.

[9]   *Freedom*, September 1895.

[10]   *Le Temps, op.cit.*

[11]   Nellie Shaw, Whiteway: A Colony on the Cotswolds, (London, 1935), p.22.

[12]   *Newcastle Daily Chronicle,* 17 May 1894.

[13]   *The Socialist: Organ of the Sunderland Independent Labour Party*, 12 June 1894.

[14]   *Le Temps, op.cit.*

[15]   *Ibid.*

[16]   *Newcastle Daily Chronicle,* 29 January 1896.

[17]   *Le Temps, op.cit.*

[18]   *Sunderland Daily Echo*, 5 April 1895.

[19]   *Le Temps, op.cit.*

[20]   *Newcastle Daily Chronicle*, 20 February 1895.

[21]   *Sunderland Herald and Daily Post*, 22 March 1895.

[22]   *The Socialist, op.cit.* William Morris (1834–1896) was a socialist 'giant' of late-nineteenth century English art and design. Stressing that socialism was as much about the liberation of human artistic and emotional expression as changing economic systems, Morris became a prominent figure in the 'revival' of socialism in the 1880s, playing an active part in the Democratic Federation and later the Socialist League and the Hammersmith Socialist Society. His books, and notably *News From Nowhere* (1890), echoed

32

Kropotkin's views on the organisation of a future socialist society and were extremely popular. See: E.P. Thompson, *William Morris: Romantic to Revolutionary,* (London, 1977); Philip Henderson, *William Morris: His Life, Work and Friends,* (New York, 1967); Paul Thompson, *The Work of William Morris,* (New York, 1967); Fiona MacCarthy, *William Morris: A Life for Our Time,* (London 1994), and *Anarchy and Beauty: William Morris and His Legacy, 1860–1960,* (London, 2014).

[23] *Sunderland Herald and Daily Post,* 22 March 1895.

[24] *Ibid.,* 19 March 1895.

[25] *Ibid.,* 22 March 1895.

[26] *Ibid.,* 27 March 1895.

[27] *Ibid.,* 28 March 1895.

[28] *Ibid.,* 4 April 1895.

[29] *Ibid.,* 5 April 1895.

[30] *Ibid.*

[31] *Weekly Times and Echo,* 3 May–19 July 1896. Arthur Baker had visited several of the American communist communities. There is a short biographical note in Shaw, *op.cit.,* pp.28–29.

[32] See: Harvey O'Connor, *Revolution in Seattle,* (Seattle, 1981 edn).

[33] See particularly: *Seedtime: Organ of the New Fellowship,* 1893–1895. There are numerous references to Colonia Cosme in the labour press of the 1890s.

[34] Useful summaries of the motivations behind land colonies, and the experience of individual communities can be found in: Charlotte Alston, *op.cit.* Dennis Hardy, *Alternative Communities in Nineteenth Century England,* (New York, 1979); Jan Marsh, *Back to the Land,* (London, 1982); W.H.G. Armytage, *Heavens Below: Utopian Experiments in England 1560–1960,* (London, 1961); M.J. De K. Holman, 'The Purleigh Colony: Tolstoyan togetherness in the late 1890s' in Malcolm Jones (ed), *New Essays on Tolstoy,* (London, 1978); W.H.G. Armytage, 'J.C. Kenworthy and the Tolstoyan Communities in England', in W. Gareth Jones (ed), *Tolstoi and Britain,* (Oxford/Washington DC, 1995); Matthew James Thomas, *Paths to Utopia: Anarchist Countercultures in late Victorian and Edwardian Britain, 1880–1914,* unpublished PhD thesis, University of Warwick, 1998; The Aylmer Maude papers at the University of Leeds Library (Special Collections) include copies of *The New Order.*

[35] For references to the Starnthwaite Colony see note 34 (above) and Shelia Rowbotham, 'Edward Carpenter: Prophet of the New Life' in S. Rowbotham and J. Weeks, *Socialism and the New Life*, (London, 1977); L. Thompson, *The Enthusiasts: A Biography of John and Katharine Bruce Glasier,* (London, 1971).

[36] Joy Thacker, *Whiteway Colony: The Social History of a Tolstoyan Community,* (Whiteway, Stroud, 1993); Shaw, *op.cit.* Armytage, *op.cit.*

[37] For a detailed treatment of the Owenite communities see: S. Pollard, 'Nineteenth Century Co-operation: From Community Building to Shopkeeping' in A Briggs and J. Saville, *Essays in Labour History,* (London, 1967 edn); G.D.H. Cole, *Century of Co-operation,* (Manchester, 1944); A.E. Musson, 'The Idea of Early Co-operation in Lancashire and Cheshire' in *Transactions of the Lancashire and Cheshire Antiquarian Society*, 1958; J. Harrison, *Robert Owen and the Owenites* in Britain and America, (London, 1969); R.G. Garrett, *Co-operation and the Owenite Socialist Communities in Britain, 1825–1845*, (Manchester, 1972); Barbara Taylor, *Eve and the New Jerusalem: Socialism and Feminism in the Nineteenth Century*, (London, 1983); Ian Donnachie, *Robert Owen: Social Visionary*, (Edinburgh, 2011 edn).

[38] See: R.G. Gammage, *History of the Chartist Movement 1837–1854*, (London, 1967 reprint of original 1894 edition); A.M. Hadfield, *The Chartist Land Company,* (Newton Abbot, 1970); Malcolm Chase, *Chartism: A New History,* (Manchester, 2007); Dennis Hardy, *op.cit.*

[39] *Land and Labour: Organ of the Land Nationalisation Society*, November 1896.

[40] See: P. Thompson, *op.cit.,* p.239.

[41] *Liberty*, January 1895. There is a biographical note on E.T. Craig in Joyce Bellamy and John Saville, *Dictionary of Labour Biography*, (London, 1972), Vol.1, pp.89–93.

[42] 'An Ill-fated Colony: Story of the Clousden Hill Experiment (By One of the Colonists)' in *Co-operative News*, 19 April 1902; see also the *Northern Echo*, 7 August 1896, *Newcastle Daily Chronicle*, 21 March 1895 and *Le Temps*, *op.cit.* Kapper and Key acknowledged the debt to Craig in a postscript to the colony's Statement of Objects and Principles (1895): 'For many of the above Clauses we are indebted to the late eminent Sociologist, E.T. Craig, many of which were applied in connection with his successful Co-operative Colony at Ralahine, County Clare, Ireland.'

(Information from Heiner Becker, Institute of Social History, Amsterdam).

[43] *The Torch*, 18 May 1895.

[44] Joseph Edwards (ed), *Labour Annual: A Year Book of Social, Economic and Political Reform (for) 1896*, (London, 1895), p.172. The conference was summarised in J.A. Hobson (ed), *Co-operative Labour Upon The Land: the report of a conference upon 'Land, Co-operation and the Unemployed' held at Holborn Town Hall in October 1894*, (London, 1895).

[45] R. Garnier, *Annals of the British Peasantry*, (London, 1895), pp.427–428.

[46] Hobson, *op.cit.*, p.123.

[47] *Horticultural Review*, April 1895.

[48] *Newcastle Daily Chronicle*, 21 March 1895; Nevinson, *op.cit.*, p.123, also suggested that Edward Carpenter's ideas on a 'New Life' provided inspiration

[49] *The Torch, op.cit.*

[50] *Horticultural Review, op.cit.*

Clousden Hill in the 1890s
PHOTO: JEAN GLEGHORN

35

Chapter Two
Itinerant Jewish Glaziers

Locked in battle with the *Sunderland Post* in the spring of 1895, William Key and Frank Kapper still found time to search for a suitable site for their colony. At first they concentrated on Wearside,[1] and in late March the village of Ryhope, between Sunderland and Seaham, looked like a strong possibility.[2] But for whatever reason, nowhere could be found near Sunderland, and the search switched to the Newcastle area. Kapper returned to Newcastle and bought a bicycle on weekly instalments that he used to tour the countryside in his free time looking for a vacant farm.[3] He sent details of likely locations to Key, but every prospect ran into difficulties with property agents. After two months without positive results, Kapper advertised in the *Newcastle Daily Chronicle* for 'about 40 acres with suitable farm buildings on Tyneside or Wearside.'[4] It brought the offer of a twenty-acre farm at Clousden Hill, close to the village of Forest Hall just outside the eastern edges of Newcastle. Fifteen minutes walk from Forest Hall railway station, Clousden Hill was described by one visitor as 'peopled mainly by those people who having saved enough to live comfortably on, have built themselves houses and settled down for the rest of their life.' Moving rapidly, Kapper and Key inspected the farm and immediately took out a twenty-year lease on about eighteen acres from May 1895 at an annual rent of £60 a year underwritten by Key.[5] The 'Clousden Hill Free Communist and Co-operative Colony' began to take shape.

The foundation of an anarchist colony at Clousden Hill Farm was not exactly greeted with delight. There was 'a lot of local prejudice'[6], including a certain amount of anti-semitism. 'Jews and Anarchists were more than public opinion could take', and a group of 'itinerant Jewish farm glaziers' were apparently regarded as a threat to Forest Hall's way of life, Kapper recalled: 'At the beginning [the neighbours] didn't seem to understand us. They had a strong objection to our working on Sundays, and the boys used to come shouting around the place: Who killed Christ?, evidently taking us for Jews.'[7] Luckily, Kapper could rely on a few friends and sympathisers. The land owner was a 'sympathetic' retired Newcastle solicitor, Mr. Punshon, who owned most of the land locally. The colony's landlady, Mrs. Punshon, was similarly helpful and lent plants, rose bushes, bees and other items.[8] Ben Glover, who spent a lot of time at Clousden Hill as a boy, said that his father, Walter Glover, who lived at nearby Hazelrigg, had supported the colonists: 'Walter Glover was the first they made contact with. At that time my father was one of the very first that was a member of the ILP and he was many times boycotted for his views.'[9]

As at Sunderland, the Newcastle ILP was highly active in 1895. The city's branches contested the general election held that year, operated a Labour Club in Pilgrim Street, and had formed a Women's Labour Association. Additionally, a branch of the Labour Church had been launched in February, and efforts were made by its members to open a correspondence class connected with the Labour Church magazine, the *Labour Prophet*. These developments, together with the local Fabian Society's lectures on Walt Whitman, the American apostle of free life styles, were not without relevance for Kapper and his group. The fact that Newcastle socialists embraced what was known at the time as 'the philosophy of the New Life'[10] implied that they were disposed to welcome the Clousden Hill colony. This openness towards anarchism was given a mild boost when the ILP's national conference met at Newcastle's Geographical Institute in April 1895. The conference deleted a clause in the Party's constitution prohibiting 'action as may in any way associate' the ILP and anarchists.[11] Whilst not suggesting any positive approval of anarchism, reflecting simply an

37

unwillingness to 'throw stones' at anarchists, the deletion of the clause at least eased co-operation between ILPers and anarchists.

Another advantage in Newcastle was the attitude of the press. The city's Liberal and Tory newspapers completely ignored the colony, representing a definite improvement on the *Sunderland Post*. But more importantly, there was even supportive coverage from the *Newcastle Daily Chronicle*, which itself had a link with Kropotkin. The *Newcastle Daily Chronicle,* 'parent' of Tyneside's present-day *Chronicle* daily newspaper, now part of the Trinity Mirror Group, was a newspaper triumph of the nineteenth-century. Under the proprietorship of the fiercely independent Radical Member of Parliament, Joseph Cowen, the paper achieved a large-scale circulation serviced by the latest printing technology, energetic editors (including W.E. Adams who had once been notorious for advocating the right to assassinate tyrants!), and politics dedicated to championing labour rights, Irish Home Rule and almost every struggle for liberty and justice at home and abroad. Cowen built a formidable Radical position in the North East that challenged not only the Tories but the Liberal Party as well. He readily identified with 'advanced' Causes including, at least initially, the Democratic Federation (forerunner of the Social-Democratic Federation). Although Cowen, in common with a good few other Radicals, veered towards a jaundiced view of independent working-class movements and became an Imperialist in the latter stages of his life, his previous record was not forgotten. So close had been Cowen's affinity with revolutionary politics that the SDF newspaper, *Justice*, carried a glowing tribute when he died in 1900: 'Revolutionists of all countries will join with us in mourning the death of Joseph Cowen... the sturdy champion of oppressed peoples everywhere.'[12]

Peter Kropotkin was one of Cowen's many associates. Cowen's opposition to Tsarist rule opened the pages of the *Chronicle* to Kropotkin, as well as verbatim reports of his speeches on Russia delivered from public platforms such as the Durham Miners' Gala. The *Chronicle* became the one major daily newspaper in Europe available to Kropotkin, and it reported his frequent visits to Newcastle in the 1880s and 1890s when he lectured to packed audiences that included the Tyneside Sunday Lecture Society. Through the links with Kropotkin, anarchism could also count on a comparatively fair hearing from the *Chronicle*. When the French anarchist, Martial Bourdin, blew himself up as he was carrying a bomb through Greenwich Park in February 1894, sparking a 'law and order' frenzy in the press and the banning of the Autonomie Club, the *Chronicle* kept a cool head and bravely published two major editorials placing the blame for anarchist violence squarely at the door of a repressive French government that drove people to desperate measures.[13] Meanwhile, the newspaper reported favourably on the contents of what it described as the 'beautifully printed' and 'literary' magazine, *Torch*, produced by the London anarchist Rossetti sisters.

The *Chronicle* was the first paper, ahead even of the anarchist journals, to publish Kropotkin's thoughts on Kapper's and Key's colony. Despite turning down the invitation to act as treasurer, Kropotkin was sufficiently interested to visit in February 1896, offering extensive advice, and presenting a book on horticulture inscribed: 'To the comrades of the young colony with heartiest good wishes and best sympathies, P. Kropotkin.'[14] In general terms, he 'had little confidence in schemes of communistic communities started under present conditions', preferring anarchists to conduct propaganda among the masses. Kropotkin warned about dangers posed by insufficient funds, influxes of too many newcomers at times of prosperity, any failure to appreciate the need for hard work, and the limited social life in small colonies. He was not entirely negative. 'By no means should I like to discourage you and your comrades,' he wrote to Kapper and Key. 'Your scheme undoubtedly has several points,

[7-5-95]

Fr. Klapper 9 Randolph Str.
Sunderland.

ⓈⒼ N.

Dear Comrade. Excuse my delay in replying, I was rather busy lately. I hereby enclosed the desired "Loaflets" and if the time should permit you I would be much gratified by your sending me your opinions about it; Our object in issuing the "Statements of Principles & Appeal" was to find some sympathisers so as to be able to start whith about 80 members or even more, but as there are aparently none, we have as usualy rely on ourselfes and start, this allready hard task whith the resources that are in the reach of a few workmen, as sun as a suitable piece of Land whith on Cotage or two is found. The letter from Com. Krapathin was not separately published and appeared first in the "Newcastle Chronicle". The same paper has given us some valuable help on more than on occasion.

Yours for the Cause
Fr. Klapper.

which undoubtedly give it more chance of success than most previous experiments.' He then praised the 'wise decision of starting intensive culture under the guidance of experienced gardeners.' And he suggested that successful communities should be located near to colonists' home areas to avoid social isolation, and that barrack-style living should be avoided in favour of separate families. Colonies should also reject internal authority structures. Seeing the proposed colony as founded on vital principles, he stressed the importance of a further condition:

'Do all possible for reducing household work to the lowest minimum... In most communities this point was awfully neglected. The women and the girls remained in the new society as they were in the old — slaves of the community. Arrangements to reduce as much as possible the incredible amount of work which women uselessly spend in the rearing-up of children, as well as in the household work, are, in my opinion, as essential to the success of the community as the proper arrangement of the fields, the greenhouses, and the agricultural machinery. Even more. But while every community dreams of having the most perfect agricultural or industrial machinery; it seldom pays attention to the squandering of the forces of the house slave, the women.'[15]

Anarchist-communism, explained Kropotkin, was committed to abolishing the exploitation of women and to seek their liberation from domestic drudgery. Technology, he believed, would reduce the burden of household chores and that would help to free women. But a far-reaching alteration in male attitudes was absolutely essential. As he wrote in *The Conquest of Bread*: 'Servant or wife, man always reckons on women to do the housework. But woman, too, at last claims her share in the emancipation of humanity. She no longer wants to be the beast of burden of the house... Why has woman's work never been of any account? ... Because those who want to emancipate mankind have not included women in their dream of emancipation, and consider it beneath their superior masculine dignity to think of "those kitchen arrangements" which they have layed on the shoulders of that drudge — woman... let us fully understand that a revolution, intoxicated with the beautiful words Liberty, Equality, Solidarity would not be a revolution if it maintained slavery at home. Half humanity subjected to the slavery of the hearth would still have to rebel against the other half.'[16]

Kropotkin was concerned to impress the urgency of women's freedom upon Kapper and Key, and for their part they seemed receptive enough for Kropotkin to note that 'you are agreed.'[18] Accordingly, the Clousden Hill colony's prospectus carried explicit references to women's status. The colony was 'to be regulated by a Joint Committee of all the adult male and female members.'[17] Unexceptional as this may seem, it should be remembered that this was at a time when women were more often than not excluded from membership of organisations, and even from movements dedicated to social emancipation. A number of co-operative societies on Tyneside excluded women from membership until well into the twentieth century,[19] and it was usually difficult for women to get anywhere near positions of influence in socialist organisations.

Quite how thoroughly thought out was the notion of equality to be applied in the Clousden Hill colony was less certain. The prospectus stated: 'all housework, such as cooking, cleaning, washing, etc., [was] to be done on the most improved system, to relieve the women from the long and tiresome work which unduly falls to their share today, so as to give them opportunity for leisure, and the free exercise of all their faculties.'[20] This didn't firmly pin down whether the men would actually take on a share of the domestic work. Likewise, the responsibility for looking after any children — presented in terms of 'the education of the children to be performed by competent persons'[21] — did not specify who would have primary responsibility (the women or the men or all the adults equally?). One clue could perhaps be implied by a reference in the prospectus to priorities in the distribution of food that might be in short supply: 'sick persons, children and women to have precedence.' Over time, the experience of women, who were always present, became clearer. Kapper claimed in 1897 that on the move to Clousden

Hill the colony had 'eleven members, of whom only three were men', though another report suggests that the women who actively took part were far fewer at the beginning.[22]

Other aspects of the colony's projected structure and operation were more definite. The venture was to be managed along strictly anarchist communist lines. There would be a secretary and a treasurer, restricted to purely administrative duties, keeping minute books and accounts, and appointed by the entire membership. All the members would form a committee to meet 'every night, if necessary, to discuss, regulate, and distribute the work among themselves, and settle any other business for the next day, or any future time.' The division of the colony's members into majorities and minorities by systems of voting, carrying dangers of producing a type of 'authority', would not be permitted. Instead, 'all fundamental points' would be 'discussed until unanimity is established' since: 'this association being constituted on the principles of Liberty and Equality, [does] not recognise any other authority than the one of Reason, and no member or members shall have any other power than that of Reasoning.' As a long-stop against any irreconcilable disagreements an arbitration clause was inserted into the colony's constitution, so that 'should any of the members have a dispute with any other person, we think it advisable to abide by the decision of any person or persons agreed to, to whom the matter in question may have been referred.'[23]

Underlying the consensual principles were assumptions of solidarity and self-discipline on the part of all the members. These assumptions were most clearly expressed in statements about work, clothing and food. The colonists agreed that: 'Whatever talents we may individually possess, whether agricultural, industrial or scientific, shall be directed to the benefit of all, by their immediate exercise in all necessary occupations: also by communicating knowledge to each other, particularly to

43

the young.' No fixed working hours would be set 'except in cases of general agreement' as: 'We believe that, considering these new conditions, each one will do his best, and work according to his abilities, physically or otherwise.' Clothing would be made as far as possible 'by the members, and supplied free to all from the common fund' with 'necessity to regulate the supply.' Food would be provided 'either in the raw state from the common store, or cooked from the common kitchen, free according to the needs of each.'[24]

The colony would sell its 'surplus production' to customers 'at a reasonable price' or would exchange goods 'for other useful articles of comfort.' Any income raised would be ploughed back into the colony, although some money would be allocated to individual members: 'For any article where the desire for such is only particular and not general, a small sum previously agreed to shall be handed over to each member weekly or monthly, as arranged, to dispose of according to his or her inclination.'[25] The emphasis on 'modern' methods of production was very evident, too. The 'whole of the land' was to be 'cultivated intensively, either as vegetable gardens or orchards', with a 'portion... covered with glass immediately, and extended as funds permit' together with the introduction of 'as many industries into the Colony as possible.'[26] Work 'whether agricultural, gardening, or industrial [would] be done on the most advanced principles of scientific research and instruction: the machines to be used wherever possible...'[27]

Equipped with high hopes and some money ('about £150 of our own money, £150 was a loan free of interest, Mr. Samuel Storey, M.P., gave us £25, and other gifts brought our total capital up to about £350' according to Kapper), the first colonists moved on to Clousden Hill Farm in May 1895. The pioneers included Kapper, as well as Robert Walker and E.T. Dipper (the former a coal miner from Boldon, and the latter a farmhand). With 'a happy belief in their own energy and common sense, and such knowledge as could be gleaned from cheap books on agriculture, poultry-rearing, &c., the tailor and the miner set to work on a calling new to them all.'[28] One newspaper report stated that six children and a number of women accompanied the men, but a more reliable account suggested that only one woman, Mrs. Walker, was there at the start. From the previous tenant, the group took over quantities of hay, oats, potatoes, fruit bushes, vegetables, '62 fowls', and agricultural tools for which they were charged £100 payable in two instalments. Kapper described the site as 'twelve acres of grass land, six acres of standing oats, and a quarter of an acre of potatoes. There was a house, barn, pig-sty, cow-byre, stable, &c.'[29]

Kropotkin's caution about the necessity of hard work proved only too true ('The oats we mowed by hand, and found it very stiff work' Kapper recalled 'grimly'). Dipper kept his old job for a while, and for the first six months Frank Kapper combined labouring on the farm with tailoring work in Sunderland, travelling on his bicycle and eating his 'ration' of bread and cheese on the way: 'One secret of our success was that two of us did not at once abandon our occupations, but came to and fro in times of leisure.' He and the other colonists were soon putting in an average of 19 hours a day, including Sundays.[30] But enthusiasm overcame any doubts in the minds of the pioneers who took 'advantage of the moonlight nights in the winter time to carry on their digging operations.' Another 'comrade' joined in October 1895 and by January there were five men 'so that when the spring came we were able to set to work in full earnest [bringing] about four acres of ground into garden state and planted it with peas (which gave a very good return), cabbages, potatoes, &c.' The farm stock was quickly increased by a cow, a goat, two pigs, twenty-two hens and chickens, six ducks, sixty-five geese, eight turkeys and two pairs of rabbits, at a total cost of £38.7s.1d. Milk sales proved to be a 'steady source of income', bringing 'in £1 a week for seven or eight weeks', the pigs proved 'remunerative', and the colonists obtained 'a fairly good price' for the geese and turkeys specially fattened for the Christmas market.[31]

Work began at once on the centrepiece of the enterprise: 'For intensive cultivation we have built a glasshouse 100 feet long by 15 feet wide, which is ready for glazing and fittings: and for forcing purposes we have constructed 4 frames.'[32] Unfortunately, the glasshouse was blown down twice during its construction,[33] and there were delays in receiving payment of 'outstanding accounts' for the Christmas geese and turkeys. Nevertheless, between October 1895 and March 1896 the colony recorded a turnover of £214, with Kapper noting: 'everything produced on the farm has met a ready sale... A cow half paid its purchase money in a few weeks: and a pig quickly appreciated by 400 per cent.' The glasshouse was rebuilt with Kapper and the others making the concrete foundations and walls and they 'purchased a sort of donkey boiler for £6, [and] fitted up the water pipes themselves.' Five hundred tomato plants produced impressive crops, some purchased by a professional gardener and others sold in Newcastle until the Sunderland co-operative society ('in the true spirit of co-operation') offered to take all the vegetables and voluntarily raised the buying price of the tomatoes from 6d a pound to 7d ('they showed their solidarity', Kapper said). The initial buoyancy enabled the colonists to begin 'scheming how to place another [glasshouse] alongside' the first one – 'glasshouses and intensive culture generally are Mr. Kapper's hobby.'[34]

Most of the colony's expenditure went on equipment, and the income reflected both sales and 'subscriptions.'[35] As it happened, the colonists were heavily dependent on 'subscriptions', or financial help from sympathisers. About £140 was raised, free of interest, in the first few months by William Key with 'a few other friends', and a further £119.16s.8d was sent by 'various London friends.'[36] The metropolitan connection included a mysterious 'wealthy London Anarchist',[37] together with 'Mrs Dryhurst and Mr. Nevinson (£8) and a little help from the Hammersmith Socialist Society' — Nannie Dryhurst being an editor of *Freedom* and Henry Nevinson was her lover and a Victorian rising journalist interested in anarchism, monetarily, through their affair.[38] Several other London anarchists also took a good deal of interest. Slipping away from his Scotland Yard 'shadow' in the autumn of 1895, the exiled German anarchist Bernard Kampffmeyer[39] visited Kapper and his comrades. On returning to London, Kampffmeyer wrote to *Freedom* urging further financial assistance:

'FREE COMMUNIST AND CO-OPERATIVE FARM NEAR NEWCASTLE.

Receiving a letter from one of the founders of this Colony I became curious to have a look at it and resolved to go there. All that I saw there seemed to me very interesting: the men appeared to be skilful, practical, industrious, and to possess the essential quality of being able to agree with each other. In short, the general conditions promise a success in my opinion.'[40]

The progress made by Kapper and the other colonists quickly brought commendations when Kapper issued a positive report in March 1896. *Freedom* believed the colony 'to be one of the most hopeful undertakings that has even been seen in these islands.'[41] *The Torch* was similarly complimentary: 'We can only say that we wish it every success and friends who are interested in agricultural experiments cannot do better than support it.'[42] And the Land Nationalisation League's organ, *Land and Labour*, although considering it 'much too soon to forecast the ultimate result of the experiment', thought 'it is worthwhile to record what has already been done, as an encouragement to others.'[43] The *Clarion* and other labour

47

Free Communist and Co-operative Colony.

Clousden Hill Farm, Forest Hall,

Newcastle-on-Tyne,

February 8th 1896

Dear Comerade

I beg to enclose our
Balance sheet & Raport which
I hope will be of interest
to you.

Trusting you will da yours
best in assisting us in our
effords

I remain yours
for the Cause
Fr. Kapper.

Frank Kapper: Apeal for funds sent to the anarchist Max
Nettlau
INTERNATIONAL INSTITUTE OF SOCIAL HISTORY, AMSTERDAM.

Mr.

1. Netlow

2 Fortune gate Terrace

Willesden

London N. W.

16

newspapers carried details of Kapper's first 'report and balance sheet', fermenting a rush of applications to join the colony. Taking Kropotkin's advice about the dangers posed by large influxes of members, the applications were 'held over to await the results from the land and the glasshouse.'[44] Meanwhile, Kropotkin made his visit. In January 1896 he spoke on land cultivation at Newcastle's Tyneside Sunday Lecture Society, apparently 'highly appreciated by the large audience present.'[45] During his stay he 'visited the Colony, stat[ing] that he was much gratified with what he had seen and the manner in which the farm was being worked.'[46]

Free Communism was now planted among the roses and fields of Clousden Hill.

Balance Sheet and Report of Free Communist and Co-operative Colony,

Clousden Hill Farm, Forest Hall, Newcastle.

To the Friends and Sympathisers of Land Colonisation.

With the end of December we have passed through the first five months of our existence as a Free Communist and Co-operative Colony, and with the expiration of the year we take the opportunity of submitting our accounts to our friends, and to give them thereby a clear statement of our position. We shall confine ourselves strictly to the account of the work of the Colony and its financial position, leaving our pleasures, hardships, anxieties, and troubles for more leisure time. In taking over the above place on a twenty years' lease, at an annual rental of £60, we took over from the last tenant stock consisting of hay, oats, potatoes, fruit bushes, vegetables, 32 fowls, and various agricultural implements, at the agreed price of £100. Of this sum we have up to the present paid £75, leaving a balance of £25 yet to be paid. We have increased our live stock by one cow, one goat, two pigs, 22 hens and chickens, 6 ducks, 54 geese, 8 turkeys, and two pair of rabbits, at a total cost of £38 7s 1d. The hay and oats we intend, if possible, to reserve for the feeding of the stock, which ought to be still more considerably increased. The sale of milk, which, during two months alone, amounts to £7 15s 3½, convinces us that increase in dairy stock would mean a valuable addition to our income. We fattened the geese and turkeys, and disposed of them during Christmas time at a fairly good price, a considerable portion of our outstanding accounts being part of this transaction. For intensive culture we have built a glasshouse 100 feet long by 15 feet wide, which is ready for glazing and inside fittings; and for forcing purposes we have constructed four frames, besides which many other improvements have been made. On the whole we are more than satisfied with the results of our efforts, and the same general satisfaction has been expressed by numerous visitors, including Krapotkine, Kampffmeyer, Tom Mann, and other well-known reformers. The sum of £140 16s, free of interest, has been advanced to us in our financial struggles by our hon. treasurer, Mr William Key, and a few other friends, while through the efforts of various London friends we have received subscriptions amounting to £19 16s 8d in aid of our objects. The total of our income is £214 14s 8½d, and expenditure £213 3s 1d, leaving a small balance of £1 11s 7½d in hand. This and our outstanding accounts, amounting to £29 5s, is about the sum which will be needed for finishing and fitting up the glasshouse. Our membership for the present consists of four men, two of whom are married, and have small families; but with better resources at our disposal the number could be considerably increased. The number of applications for membership which we have received clearly shows the desire of workers to return to the land, and demonstrates the necessity of Agricultural Colonies similar to our own. However, before any further extension out of our own resources could be thought of, at least a few months must elapse so as to enable us to obtain some results from the land and glasshouse. During that time practical help from our friends will be much required, and we hope that amongst the sympathisers with our objects the appeal for aid will not be in vain. We in return give the assurance that no efforts will be spared in order to make the Colony a complete success. Any contributions can be sent to the hon. treasurer, Mr W. KEY, Tavistock House, Sunderland, and will be duly acknowledged.

F. KAPPER, Hon. Secretary.

ASSETS.

			£	s.	d.
Stock of Hay...	...	...	35	0	0
„ Straw	...	...	10	0	0
„ Oats	...	...	12	10	0
„ Potatoes	...	...	4	0	0
„ Fruit Bushes and Rhubarb			15	0	0
Implements and Tools ...		...	20	0	0
Fowls	...	...	8	10	0
Pigs	...	...	6	0	0
Cow and Goat	...	...	20	0	0
Wood	...	...	4	10	0
Rabbits	...	...	1	5	0
Fowl Houses...	...	...	3	0	0
Greenhouse as it stands...		...	60	0	0
Frames	...	...	3	0	0
General Improvements ...		...	15	0	0
Manure	...	...	5	0	0
Money in hand	...	...	1	11	7½
Outstanding Accounts	...	...	29	5	0
			253	11	7½

LIABILITIES.

			£	s.	d.
Owing to Stock	...	...	25	0	0
To Friends ...	...	...	140	16	0
Total Liabilities...		...	165	16	0

			£	s.	d.
Total Income ...	...		214	14	8½
Total Expenditure	...		213	3	1
Balance in hand ...			1	11	7½

Examined, compared and found correct,

J. W. KEY.
T. FOSTER WATTS.

INCOME.

				£	s.	d.
July 24th, Messrs Wm. Key and B. Smyrke	...	...		20	0	0
" 25th, Mr F. Kapper	...	...	...	3	0	0
Aug. 9th, Mr F. Kapper	...	...	...	7	13	6
" 9th, Mr R. Walker	...	...	...	20	0	0
" 26th, C. Porter	...	...	...	3	4	0
From Fowls...	...	...	...	1	0	3
" Farm ...	...	...	...	0	3	6
Total income for July and August ...		...	...	55	1	3
Sept. 28th, Messrs W. Key and B. Smyrke...	...	...		30	0	0
" " R. Walker	...	...	...	5	0	4½
From Fowls...	...	...	...	0	10	9
" Farm ...	...	...	...	1	1	11½
Total for September ...	...	—	...	36	13	1
Oct. 5th, Mr C. Porter...	...	...	...	1	13	8
" 23rd, Mr W. Key	...	...	...	24	6	0
" 24th, Mr W. Key	...	...	...	16	0	0
From Farm	...	...	...	2	19	0½
" Fowls	...	...	...	0	8	6
Total for October	...	...	...	45	7	2½
Nov. 9th, Mr C. Porter ...	...	...	...	1	5	11
" " Subscriptions through Mrs Dayhurst & Mr Nevinson				8	0	0
" " Mr B. Kampftmeyer (subscription)		...	...	4	0	0
" " Miss Ridley (subscription)...	...	...	...	5	0	0
" " Mr Menil (subscription)	...	...	...	1	11	8
" " Mr F. Kapper	...	...	...	2	0	0
" " Shields Friend (subscription)	...	...	...	0	10	0
" 27th Mr W. Key	...	...	...	1	10	0
" 29th, R. Walker	...	...	...	5	10	0
" " C. Porter	...	...	...	1	10	10
From Milk	...	...	...	3	0	5
" Farm	...	...	...	1	16	0
Total for November ...	...	...	...	35	14	10
Dec. 7th, A Friend	...	...	...	30	0	0
" 27th, F. Kapper	...	...	...	2	10	0
From Milk	...	...	...	4	14	10½
" Farm	...	...	...	0	10	0½
" Fowls	...	...	...	0	2	0
" Geese	...	...	...	3	6	5
Through Mrs Dayhurst	...	...	...	0	15	0
Total for December ...	...	...	...	41	18	4
July and August ...	...	...		55	1	3
September	...	...		36	13	1
October ...	...	...		45	7	2½
November...	...	...		35	14	10
December...	...	...		41	18	4
Total Income	...	...		214	14	8½

EXPENDITURE.

		£	s.	d.
July 25th, First Payment to Stock on Farm		20	0	0
Aug. 7th, Removals		4	18	0
,, 4th, Seeds		0	8	3½
,, 7th, Fowls and Rabbits		4	6	0
,, 22nd, Carriage and Stacking of hay		1	19	6
,, ,, Wood and Carriage		0	19	0
,, ,, Fowl Houses		2	15	0
,, 26th, Two Pigs		1	18	0
,, ,, Straw for Thatching		1	3	6
,, ,, Goat		0	15	0
,, ,, Food of Stock		0	17	4½
,, ,, Tools and Implements		1	0	11
Total for July and August		41	0	7
Sept. 28th, Second Payment on account of Stock ...		40	0	0
,, ,, Ducks, Geese, and Carriage		1	7	0
,, ,, Food of Stock		1	8	5
Total for September		42	15	5
Oct. 3rd, Carriage and Stacking of Oats		1	0	0
,, 5th, Nails and Bolts		1	7	1
,, 23rd, Wood and leading of same		24	14	0
,, 26th, Geese, Turkeys, Rabbits and Carriage ...		11	11	1
,, 29th, Thrashing of Oats		3	2	6
,, ,, Tools and Implements		0	8	0
,, ,, Food of Stock		2	8	8
Total for October		44	11	4
Nov. 9th, Bolts		0	6	3
,, 9th, Cow		15	0	0
,, 12th, Churn and Milk Utensils		1	7	7
,, ,, Glass and Putty		0	5	6
,, ,, Rent and Water Rate		15	2	8
,, ,, Coals from July		1	13	6
,, ,, Sevens Load of Stone		0	10	6
,, ,, Two Loads of Lime		1	0	0
,, ,, 2,250 Bricks and Carriage... ...		3	5	3
,, ,, Tools and Implements		1	1	3
,, ,, Railway Fare and Postage ...		0	7	6
,, ,, Food for Stock		3	0	5
,, ,, Groceries and Provisions		0	19	7
Total for November		44	0	0
Dec. 7th, Third Payment on account of Stock ...		15	0	0
,, ,, Balance on account of Cow ...		3	10	0
,, 19th, Boiler		6	0	0
,, ,, Coals		0	14	1½
,, ,, Crushed Bricks and Carriage ...		0	13	0
,, ,, Cement and Carriage		2	11	2
,, ,, Tools and Implements		0	18	9½
,, ,, Carriage of Geese		1	3	0
,, ,, Postage		0	3	0
,, ,, Food of Stock		5	2	8
,, ,, House Expenses		5	0	0
Total for December		40	15	9
July and August		41	0	7
September...		42	15	5
October		44	11	4
November		44	0	0
December		40	15	9
		213	3	1

References

[1] *Newcastle Daily Chronicle,* 20 February 1895.

[2] *Sunderland Daily Echo,* 23 March 1895.

[3] *Le Temps, op.cit.*

[4] *Newcastle Daily Chronicle,* 24 April 1895.

[5] *Le Temps, op.cit.* Northern Echo, 7 August 1896.

[6] 'Co-operation and the Land: Visit to a Communistic Colony' in *Co-operative News,* 26 February 1898.

[7] *Le Temps,* op. cit; *Northern Echo,* 11 August 1896.

[8] *Le Temps,* ibid; *Northern Echo,* 7 August 1896.

[9] Cited in Armytage, *op.cit.,* p.313.

[10] Rowbotham, *op.cit.*

[11] *Newcastle Evening Chronicle,* 16 April 1894.

[12] *Justice,* 24 February 1900. For details of Cowen's life see: Nigel Todd, *The Militant Democracy: Joseph Cowen and Victorian Radicalism,* (Whitley Bay, 1991); Joan Allen, *Joseph Cowen and Popular Radicalism on Tyneside, 1829–1900,* (Monmouth, 2007); Bellamy and Saville, *op.cit.,* vol. 1., pp.81–86. W.E. Adams wrote an autobiography, *Memoirs of a Social Atom,* (London, 1903), 2 vols. It is a vivid account of many of the revolutionary movements of the nineteenth-century — Chartism, European nationalism, Anarchism — as seen through the eyes of a radical newspaperman. The 'Tyrannicide affair' is recounted in detail, and revolved around a celebrated court case in 1858. The British Government, under French pressure, attempted to prosecute Adams and his publisher for a pamphlet entitled, *Tyrannicide: Is it Justifiable?* Adams wrote the pamphlet in defence of an attempted assassination of Louis Napoleon. The Government's action shocked radical opinion that rallied to Adams' defence (among those contributing to his 'defence fund' were John Stuart Mill and Joseph Cowen). See: Adams, op. cit., vol 2, pp.352–372; Owen Ashton, *W.E.Adams: Chartist, Radical and Journalist (1832–1906),* (Whitley Bay, 1991), pp.74–78; Bellamy and Saville, *op.cit.,* (1984), vol. 7., pp.1–4.

[13] *Newcastle Daily Chronicle,* 19 February and 22 February, 1894.

[14] Kropotkin gave Kapper and Key permission to publish his letter. It appeared in the *Newcastle Daily Chronicle* on 20 February 1895; the first anarchist journal to publish the

letter was *Liberty* in March 1895. In a letter to the anarchist, Max Nettlau, Kapper noted that the *Newcastle Daily Chronicle* had given 'valuable help on more than one occasion' (Kapper to Nettlau, 7 May 1895: Nettlau Collection, International Institute of Social History, Amsterdam); see also *Northern Echo, op.cit.*

[15] *Newcastle Daily Chronicle*, 20 February 1895.

[16] P. Kropotkin, *The Conquest of Bread*, (London, 1906 edn), pp.161,165–166.

[17] *Newcastle Daily Chronicle, op.cit.*

[18] *Torch*, 18 May 1895.

[19] Florence Cowings, a former member of the National Executive Committee of the Co-operative Women's Guild, and secretary of the Guild's Winlaton branch for many years, told the author how she had led a campaign in the 1930s to change the rules of the Blaydon Co-operative Society so that women could join in their own right. Most of the larger societies changed their rules to allow what was called 'open membership' in the 1890s and the first two decades of the twentieth century, but the Co-operative Women's Guild usually had to bring pressure to bear on the men for this to happen. See: Cole, *op.cit.,* pp.184, 220–221; Jean Gaffin and David Thomas, *Caring & Sharing: The Centenary History of the Cooperative Women's Guild* (Manchester, 1983), pp.18–19. The Blaydon Co-operative Society, at its foundation in 1858 (the first 'modern' co-operative society to be established in the North East), had been intended as a 'model' for others to emulate on Tyneside. See: Bellamy and Saville, *op.cit.,* vol. 1., p.83; Joan Hugman, 'Joseph Cowen and the Blaydon Co-operative Society: A North East Model' in Bill Lancaster and Paddy Maguire, *Towards the Co-operative Commonwealth: Essays in the History of Co-operation*, (Manchester, 1996).

[20] *Torch, op.cit.*

[21] *Ibid.*

[22] *Le Temps, op.cit. Northern Echo*, 11 and 29 August 1896.

[23] *Torch, op.cit.* Tolstoyans also adopted the unanimity principle at the Purleigh Colony and subsequently at Whiteway.

[24] *Ibid.*

[25] *Ibid.*

[26] *Liberty*, May 1895.

[27] *Torch, op.cit.*

28 *Co-operative News*, 19 April 1902; *Le Temps*, op. cit; *Northern Echo*, 7 August 1896.

29 *Northern Echo*, 29 August 1896, quotes Mrs. Walker confirming that she was the only woman at the colony at the start; *Clarion*, 22 February 1896.

30 *Le Temps, op.cit. Northern Echo, op.cit.*

31 *Clarion*, 22 February 1896; *Northern Echo*, 7 August 1896.

32 *Clarion, op.cit.*

33 *Newcastle Daily Chronicle*, 13 February 1896; *Northern Echo, op.cit.*

34 *Newcastle Daily Chronicle,* ibid; *Northern Echo, op.cit.*

35 *Freedom*, March 1896.

36 *Newcastle Evening Chronicle*, 12 February 1896.

37 W.C. Hart, *Confessions of an Anarchist*, (London, 1906), p.77.

38 *Freedom, op.cit.* For biographical notes on Nannie Dryhurst (1856–1930) see: Hermia Oliver, *The International Anarchist Movement in Late Victorian London*, (London, 1983), p.156, and https://libcom.org/history/dryhurst-nannie-florence-1856–1930

39 Bernard Kampffmeyer (1867–1942) had been active on the left-wing of the German Social-Democratic Party but became an anarchist. He contributed to the *Torch* in 1894, and spent time in the Channel Islands studying intensive horticulture (Kropotkin visited him there). Kampffmeyer apparently had a good deal of money that he used to support anarchist projects. He ceased to be an anarchist after 1900 and turned to founding the German garden cities movement. The Home Office received police reports on Kampffmeyer and his contacts. See: 'Foreign Anarchists Visiting the UK, 1892–1906' in Home Office Papers HO/144/587/B2840C (17 April 1894).

40 *Freedom*, October 1895.

41 *Ibid.*

42 *Torch*, 1 March 1896.

43 *Land and Labour*, March 1896.

44 *Newcastle Evening Chronicle, op.cit.*

45 *Newcastle Daily Journal,* 31 January 1896.

46 *Newcastle Daily Chronicle, op.cit.*

A COMMUNIST COLONY.

CLOUSDEN HILL FARM.

[BY OUR SPECIAL COMMISSIONER.]

Properly speaking, the land belongs to these two':
To the Almighty God, and to all His children of men
that have ever worked well on it, or that shall ever
work well on it.

It is the strange product of the present age that
on the one side we have complaints about agricultural depression and land going out of cultivation, and on the other side men and women in our
great cities dying of hunger, and a system of food
importation that has to be paid heavily for in the
shape of a powerful fleet to keep the supremacy of
the seas lest our outside food supply being cut off
the whole country, and not alone the submerged
tenth, be face to face with starvation. Here is
the immediate problem—the land wanting culti-
vators, the people starving, or shortening their
lives in occupations which they would gladly
exchange for the more healthful and congenial
calling of agriculture if they only knew how to do
so. Difficulties? Yes, the position has its
difficulties ; but amidst the labour congresses
that come to nothing and the profitless discussions of various schools of thinkers as to the
remedy, it is pleasant to have met with a body of
men who have made up their minds as to what
can be done and have done it. Let me describe
a visit I paid a day or two ago to the Clousden
Farm Colony at Forest Hall, near Heaton, where
a band of men and women, with their children,
are endeavouring to readjust the conditions of
existence into more harmonious relations with
themselves.

Clousden Farm is easily reached from Forest
Hall Station. Forest Hall itself is a growing
village, peopled mainly by those who having
saved enough to live comfortably on, have built
themselves houses and settled down for the rest
of life. Much of the land, Clousden Farm included, is owned by Mr Punshon, a Newcastle
solicitor, now retired. On leaving the station, a
quarter of an hour's walk brought me to Clousden,
and the house that shelters most of the inmates of
the colony was pointed out by a kindly resident,
who also warned me to beware of the dog at the
gate, as she believed he was savage. This I found
to be a libel, for "Jack," the handsome retriever
in question, has a better disposition than some
humans.

The great merit in a visit of inspection, such as
mine was to be, is its unforeseen character. I
found the women of the community washing ; the
men engaged in weeding and other occupations
necessary to the oversight of four or five acres of
garden ground. I was the bearer of a letter of
introduction from Councillor Bell, of Sunderland,
a firm friend of the colonists, and having this I
was at once made welcome. Inquiring for Mr F.
Kapper, or, as Councillor Bell had addressed
him, "Comrade" Kapper, I was conducted to
the tomato house. My guide was a Nottingham
shoemaker, who expressed to me as we went
along the pleasure it had given him to leave his
old occupation and throw in his lot with the
colony. He had brought with him £60, and
added it to the capital of the colonists.

A few words about Comrade Kapper, the
originator of the colony, may not be out of place.
Born in the town of Schlan, near Prague, what
are called on the Continent revolutionary doc-
trines found an active propagandist in him, and
if the authorities had had cognisance of his connection with several secret imprimeries penal
servitude would have been his lot. Coming to
this country eight or nine years ago he found in
London congenial spirits in the Anarchist clubs,
but none, I venture to think, rivalling himself in
the intense belief in the principles of communism
and in the earnestness with which he endeavoured
to circulate them. He was the founder of and
active spirit in the Autonomic Club, whose windows
during the Anarchist scare in London were
smashed by students. Coming northward he
worked for three years in Newcastle, and
three years in Sunderland as ladies' tailor
at Corder's. He admitted that it was the
absurdity of a strong, healthy man like himself
being employed at a confined occupation, and as
he quaintly put it, "working almost to deform
women instead of helping them," that con-
duced to his resolve to break with such
a life altogether. The conception of the
practicability of a communistic colony belongs to the time when he was a member of
the Newcastle Workmen's Educational Club, and
taught a French class. He gave the students
Krapotkin's pamphlets to translate, and one on
agriculture set him seriously thinking. A publication by the eminent sociologist, E. T. Craig,
describing the Ralahine settlement, County
Clare, in Ireland, an attempt 60 years ago to
carry out a farm settlement scheme threw still
further light on the subject, and practically decided his action.

Whilst we stood in the tomato house admiring
the splendid fruit produced by the Excelsior,
General Grant, and Perfection varieties, Mr
Kapper related the conditions under which he,
Comrade Walker, a Boldon miner, and Comrade Dipper first set to work. Their landlord,
who all through has been sympathetic with their
aims and objects, gave them twenty years lease
of 18 acres of land, at a rental of £30 a year ;
they entered on the ground in May last year, and
with a happy belief in their own energy and common sense, and such knowledge as could be
gleaned from cheap books on agriculture, poultry-
rearing, &c., the tailor and the miners set to work
on a calling new to them all. Later, the adven-
turers were joined by others, until now the colony
consists of nine men, four women, and thirteen
children.

Northern Echo, 7
August 1896

"We had," said Mr Kapper to me, "about 150 of our own money, £150 was a loan free of interest, Mr Samuel Storey, M.P., gave us £25, and other gifts brought our total capital up to about £350. The holding consisted of twelve acres of grass land, six acres of standing oats, and a quarter of an acre of potatoes. There was a house, barn, pig-sty, cow-byre, stable, &c., and we took over for £100 the stock, implements, standing crop of oats, and the hay crop. The latter was cut, and we only had to stack it. The oats we mowed by hand, and found it very stiff work," and Mr Kapper smiled grimly at the recollection of it.

"One secret of our success was that two of us did not at once abandon our occupations, but came to and fro in times of leisure. I used to bicycle from Sunderland, twelve miles away. We did what we could in the way of breaking up the ground with the spade for garden purposes. In November we purchased a cow, which paid well for herself, bringing in £1 a week for seven or eight weeks. We also fed up two pigs, a very remunerative operation on small holdings. In October we were joined by another comrade, and in January we numbered five men, so that when the spring came we were able to set to work in full earnest. Altogether we brought about four acres of ground into garden state, and planted it with peas (which gave a very good return), cabbages, potatoes, &c."

I gathered that it was the custom of these enthusiasts to take advantage of the moonlight nights in the winter time to carry on their digging operations. The ground is nicely sheltered from the north, being on a slope, at the crest of which is Killingworth Old Pit, where George Stephenson once worked. He was first a brakesman at West Moor, and went from thence to be engineman at Killingworth.

The open winter, I learnt, facilitated the work of digging somewhat, but against that advantage must be placed the high winds which blow over their glass-house, 100 feet long, by 15 feet broad. This was commenced in the autumn, but was not ready for use till the following March. The colonists made the concrete foundation and walls themselves: purchased a sort of donkey boiler for £6, fitted up the hot-water pipes themselves, and now have as fine a show of tomatoes on their 500 plants as can be found in the country. Some of the fruit has been purchased for exhibition purposes, the buyer, a professional gardener, naively remarking in his letter "As you can lick us by long chalks." But glass houses and intensive culture generally are Mr Kapper's hobby, and indeed Article 8 of the articles of association states that the object of the colony is "to demonstrate the productivity of land under intensive culture. The glass house cost £60, exclusive of labour, and they are now scheming how to place another alongside it. Till about three weeks ago the colony disposed of its vegetable produce in the best way it could, the stuff mostly going to Newcastle, but about a month ago the Sunderland Co-operative Society made an arrangement to take all the vegetables they produced. They fixed the price of their tomatoes at 6d per lb.; the Co-operative Society, in the true spirit of co-operation, voluntarily advanced that figure to 7d, "in which," as Mr Kapper quaintly remarked, "they showed their solidarity." Good word, solidarity.

Leaving the glass-house, we proceeded to view the vegetable beds, stretched out in long rows before us. Being broken land, there is a constant struggle with the weeds.

"We are tremendously bothered with them," said my guide; "we burn them by the waggon load."

One of the colonists rose from his planting as we approached, and Mr Kapper discussed with him the advisability of cross planting the bed with lettuce till the other plants required the full space. This was Comrade Elders, a railway man, widower, with four daughters, also inmates of the colony. He proceeded to inform me that on Bank Holiday two brakes load of I.L.P. members from Sunderland had come over to look round the farm. As a return civility they had invited the colonists to a tea and conversazione on August 13.

"Instead of us running after pleasure," said Mr Kapper, replying to a remark of mine, "pleasure is running after us."

"How do you like the life?" I asked Mr Elders.

"I like it well enough" was the reply. "I was not used to it at first. I formerly had charge of the piece-work in the locomotive department of the North British Railway in Scotland."

"There is a man over there," said Mr Kapper humorously, "who prays every day that he may not have to go back to his former work."

"And what was that?" I queried.

"Blacksmith," said my guide sententiously, and led the way across the top of the field to where Comrade Richardson was working. A picturesque figure he looked, too, in his shirt sleeves and broad-brimmed hat. He stopped in his occupation of planting young leeks to converse. His, I learned, had been a varied life. Son of a shipowner and captain in connection with James Young & Company; he was brought up as a blacksmith; had worked in Palmer's shipyard; had been a prison warder; and served in the English and American armies. He did not think much of soldiering any way, but in his opinion it was a gentleman's life in the English army compared with his American experience."

"When you ain't fighting the Indians they put you to navvying—navvying!" he repeated with deep disgust. It evidently did not seem to him to be such utilitarian work as small holdings cultivation.

(To be continued.)

Chapter Three
Visitors and Rivals

Peter Kropotkin and Bernard Kampffmeyer were not the only people who made their way to Clousden Hill in those early months. The Bishop of Newcastle promised to visit, as did the German land reformer Michael Flurscheim, author of *Rent, Interest and Wages*. There were also several popular trade union and socialist speakers who often toured Tyneside at the tail-end of the nineteenth-century. For them, Clousden Hill was a welcome overnight stopping place. Fiery 'agitators' like Tom Mann praised the colonists for turning 'principles to action' and 'used to come and stay a few days' (evidently not sharing George Bernard Shaw's dismissive stricture that there were two kinds of socialist, 'one to sit among the dandelions and the other to organise the docks').[1] The ILP propagandists Katherine St. John Conway and Bruce Glasier stayed as well.[2] They had a soft spot for Kropotkin, whom they visited shortly after their marriage in 1893 to be treated to his views on capitalist democracy, Russian torture and his ambition 'to grow oranges and lemons and bananas as well as tomatoes, just to prove how wonderfully full of colour we could make the coal-mining areas if only we gave the miners full opportunity to use the coal they bring up from the depths.'[3] Likewise, Harry Snell, later a junior minister in the 1929 Labour government and, as chairman of the London County Council in 1938, a strong advocate of the London Gardens Society, stayed at Clousden Hill whilst giving Fabian lectures on Tyneside 'when he had hardly a pair of boots on his feet.'[4] Snell, too, had been deeply inspired by Kropotkin, seeing him as 'a man of great learning and of singular sweetness of character.' So much so, that Snell confessed: 'I accepted from him my first cigarette, which I nevertheless abandoned as soon as his back was turned.'[5]

The ease with which socialist public figures came and went at the Clousden Hill colony was more than matched by the ordinary members of the Newcastle and Sunderland ILP branches. This was underscored when the Newcastle ILPers held an 'enjoyable' mass picnic at the colony in June 1896. Over a hundred 'visitors were shown round the farm and gardens by the Colonists, and expressed their satisfaction and delight with what they saw, and with the greenhouses in particular, one of the latter containing upwards of 500 tomato plants.' Following the tour, the ILP members and the colonists held sports, and then had tea on the grounds. A 'Comrade Hicks of Newcastle' took a photograph of everybody, but regrettably this seems to have been lost. A similar visit from 'two brakes load of ILP members from Sunderland' may also have taken place in May 1896, bringing an invitation to 'a tea and conversazione' the following August.[6]

All that summer, the close solidarity between anarchist-communists and socialists was reaching new heights. In July, an International Socialist Congress was convened in London, with delegations from many overseas parties and unions. But a concerted bid was made by a section of the Marxists and the less radical participants in the Congress to exclude the 'anti-parliamentary' anarchists. The anarchists were infuriated. Nor were the more prominent British socialist leaders all that amused, since they felt that 'comrades' of the stature of Kropotkin had a right to be heard. To emphasise the point, the anarchists held their own 'International Mass Meeting for Peace' at the same time as the Congress. Kropotkin and well-known anarchists spoke, accompanied by Tom Mann and Keir Hardie (who used the ILP's newspaper, the *Labour Leader*, to publicise the affair). Among the numerous messages of support read to the anarchist rally was one from the 'Free Communist and Co-operative Colony, Clousden Hill Farm, Newcastle' in which Frank Kapper set out the colony's position and aims: 'What we think proper and worthy of our principles, is to continue our propaganda everywhere by word and example. We are further still convinced that the example we have initiated will, in the near future, produce better fruits and create more converts than all this Congress can do. Wishing you success in your anti-parliamentary campaign.'[7]

Willing to co-operate with socialists, the anarchists at Clousden Hill were delighted when major figures in the anarchist movement called. Kropotkin and Kampffmeyer have already been mentioned, but in the summer of 1896 a towering personality in European anarchism turned up. It was Elisée Reclus who had fought in the Paris Commune of 1871. Subsequently a Professor of Comparative Geography at Brussels University, the *Labour Leader* playfully wrote that Reclus 'looked about as ferocious as the head of a successful drapery establishment.'[8] Although generally dismissive of the value of anarchist communities, Reclus took time off from political meetings around the International Congress in London to go and see Clousden Hill for himself. His reactions are unknown, but the fact that he bothered to make the trip to Newcastle at all said something about the reputation so soon achieved by the colony.[9]

More anarchists were also becoming interested in living at Clousden Hill by 1896, and gradually the restrictions that had been imposed on the admission of new members were relaxed. During the course of the year an 'R. Gunderson' joined the colony, taking on the newly-created post of 'Junior Secretary.'[10] Gunderson's identity is not clear. It could have been Rasmus Gunderson, fresh from fund-raising at the London end of Emma Goldman's campaign to free the anarchist Alexander Berkman from prison in the United States.[11] His affiliation with anarchism had been catalogued by Scotland Yard, not necessarily accurately. In response to enquiries by the Austro-Hungarian government, the Yard had prepared a secret report on Gunderson for the Home Office in 1894, describing him as: 'A tailor, a Scandinavian of birth; he was for many years a prominent supporter of the, now defunct, Club Autonomie. He was also editor of the anarchist newspaper *Die Autonomie*, which was printed in German over here, but has ceased to exist. He is a violent Anarchist... has spent some time in France and speaks French fluently.'[12] Just to make sure that Gundersdon could be recognised, the report included a description: 'Age about 50. Height 5´6˝. Complexion sallow — hair, whiskers and moustache... face emaciated... looks like a Polish Jew.'[13] Presumably, Scotland Yard thought they knew a Polish Jew when they saw one! This Gunderson would have been aged about forty-four years, but first-hand accounts by Henry Nevinson and an anonymous *Northern Echo* journalist described 'R.Gunderson' as much younger, and Ben Glover thought 'Dick Gunderson' was British. Whoever he was, Gunderson was not a long-term resident at Clousden Hill, and was unlikely to have been a 'violent' anarchist as the colony's stand on terrorism was always unequivocal: 'We seek the triumph of our Cause without violence, but through free work and voluntary consent.'[14]

The anarchists were not always in the majority at Clousden Hill and the political composition of the colonists was invariably as mixed as their occupational backgrounds. A journalist visiting Kapper in the summer of 1896 came across 'a Nottingham shoemaker' who was delighted to have escaped his former job, and had contributed £60 to the colony. He also met 'Comrade Elders' who though not used to the new life 'at first' had quickly adapted from his previous role in 'charge of the piece-work in the locomotive department of the North British Railway in Scotland.' Another joyful escapee from the industrial world was 'Comrade Richardson' who had been a blacksmith: 'A picturesque figure he looked, too, in his shirt sleeves and broad-brimmed hat. He stopped in his occupation of planting young leeks to converse. His, I learned, had been a varied life. Son of a shipowner and captain in connection with James Young & Company; he was brought up as a blacksmith; had worked in Palmer's shipyard; had been a prison warder; and served in the English and American armies. He did not think much of soldiering anyway, but in his opinion it was a gentleman's life in the English army compared with his American experience. "When you ain't fighting the Indians they put you to work navvying — navvying!" he repeated with deep disgust. It evidently did not seem to him to be such utilitarian work as small holdings cultivation.'

The same journalist (could it have been Nevinson?) provided a detailed insight into tea-time at Clousden Hill which is worth repeating at length. Coming in from their work, the colonists 'seated themselves around the table': 'Taking them according to the schools of thought they represented, there were Comrades Kapper, Gunderson, and Davies, Anarchists; Comrades Walker and Richardson, advocates of State Socialism; Comrades Brown, a Scarborough schoolmaster (he was absent on this occasion), and Bumstead, the Nottingham shoemaker, Independent Labour Party men; and Comrade Elder, a member of the Home Colonisation Association. The preparative work already accomplished on the holding has been mainly done by five men: Comrades Walker, Kapper, Dipper, Davies, and Gunderson. The others are more recent arrivals, and the last comer is Comrade Short, a man out of employment who has found refuge here. Lively discussions these men must have in the evenings, when there is a brief respite from work, and when they gather round the fire with their pipes. Even at the tea-table an energetic but perfectly good humoured discussion arose between Judge (formerly an engineer), who was one of the best speakers of the Glasgow band of Social Democrats, and Kapper, who had been connected with the Anarchist movement since 1882, as to the part the Anarchists played in the recent Congress in London.'[15]

Under the constitution, members agreed to 'admit, according to vacancies, anyone willing' to put 'Communist principles into practice as a member.' The day-to-day application of this rule came to mean that the colony was open to anyone who asked to join, bringing in its wake unexpected arrivals such as six people who 'arrived with their bundles from Newcastle' without warning early in 1896.[16] The constitution offered all members 'reasonable housing accommodation, with due regard for privacy and families.'[17] To meet the obligation, two houses were rented in Forest Hall by the middle of the year after the numbers had grown from four men, two women and several children in February to sixteen adults and eight children by August. However, the accommodation could not be expanded indefinitely, and it was announced in September that restrictions on admissions had been reimposed: 'numerous applications to join could not be dealt with, owing chiefly to lack of room.'[18]

Quite a different reason for limiting entry into the colony had meanwhile flowed from two serious problems. Firstly, Kapper and the other colonists had been joined in the spring of 1896 by a group of allegedly 'Tolstoyan Anarchists' (or, more likely, Russian Doukhobors). This group stuck firmly to the principle that everyone was 'free to work when and where' they chose. It was a different approach to work than the collectivist principles envisaged in the colony's constitution, and just how different was soon revealed when 'one planted a diminutive orchard in a most unsuitable position, another tried duck-breeding without the slightest knowledge of the subject, whilst yet another insisted that social salvation lay in rearing goats.' It was the road to a 'poverty' that generated 'friction' and 'constant disagreements.'[19]

So intense were the stresses and strains that other colonists became disillusioned. One of them, a pitman named Miller, slowly found 'that Anarchism, pure and simple, would not do for agricultural or social life. It was not possible to get work done when any man might work or not, might work as he liked, might call a halt to discuss the way in which others worked.' This was too much when set against: 'The strain of always being together, at work, and in play, feeding and sitting together... when the first glow of enthusiasm was over.'[20] Relationships went from bad to worse until, under pressure, the individualists 'gathered up their tares and penates' and emigrated to Canada.[21]

The tensions were more or less successfully concealed at the time with Frank Kapper, deploying his flair for optimism, presenting an encouraging chronicle of life at Clousden Hill. *Freedom* for example, took its cue from Kapper in March 1896, with the comment: 'The struggle will not be easy, though we are glad to see our friends facing it in cheerful and hopeful spirit.'[22] A further instance of Kapper's ability to paint a rosy picture appeared in the *Labour Leader* the following September. Kapper reported, with some licence, that the previous six months had seen 'continued extension, increase and development all round.'[23] Concentrating on positive gains, he then told *Freedom*, in October, that income had slightly exceeded expenditure since April and that four acres of market garden encompassing peas, cauliflowers, cabbages, celery and carrots had been laid out; there was now an orchard of 120 apple trees, 25 cherry trees, 2,000 berry and currant bushes, and a quarter-acre of strawberries; two-and-a-half acres of grain had been sown 'for our own use'; four acres of grass had been set aside for hay, and some land was allocated for pasture; and beekeeping together with a glasshouse containing 500 tomato plants were off to 'a good start.'[24]

Behind the public image, there was the second problem — a shortage of money to invest in the farm. In an appeal for more 'subscriptions', Kapper admitted that 'the capital at our disposal is quite inadequate.'[25] The point was picked up by the *Manchester Guardian* ('the colony was still hampered for want of capital'[26]) and the *Labour Annual* that saw Clousden Hill as 'doing well, but needs more capital.'[27] Fortunately, the colony's landlord came to the rescue in 1896 by extending the time allowed for payment of rent until after the harvest season,[28] another tribute to Kapper's persuasiveness.

On the brighter side, the colony was receiving support from the retail co-operative societies on Tyneside and Wearside. Both the Newcastle and Sunderland co-operatives bought produce from Clousden Hill, and the Sunderland co-operators donated 'a gift of £50.'[29] To some extent, relations with the co-operatives reflected a continuing mutuality of interests between anarchists and co-operators. Co-operators remained interested in land colonisation and agricultural reform, as the pages of their weekly newspaper *Co-operative News* amply testified. And the anarchists retained their affinity with Co-operation. Kropotkin wrote sympathetically on the potential of the British Co-operative Movement in the *Labour Leader* in February 1897, and later that year he published a lengthy essay on scientific farming, especially 'glasshouse culture', in the Co-operative Wholesale Societies' (CWS) prestige *Annual*.[30] For their part, the Clousden Hill colonists talked of establishing 'economic relations which comparatively approach Communism. This means close economic connection with co-operative societies, whilst conserving entirely our own autonomy.'[31]

Here again, things were not straightforward. On 20th February 1897, the *Clarion* newspaper printed a letter from R.A. Walker of High Felling (near Jarrow), unveiling a scheme for a co-operative farm. The farm would be located at Morpeth, in Northumberland, and help had been promised from the Co-operative Union (the Co-operative Movement's national advisory federation). The Jarrow co-operative society would acquire the land, and leading local co-operators had offered assistance. This proposed co-operative farm would deal in dairy produce and poultry at first, selling to co-operative stores, and 'followed at the earliest date by vegetable gardening and fruit growing ... a considerable portion of the land will be covered with glass for intensive cultivation, which portion will be increased as funds permit.'[32]

66

The idea was breathtakingly familiar to the Clousden Hill colonists, and so was Walker. 'R.A. Walker' was none other than the same Robert Walker who had been one of the original colonists. But he, Miller and Charles Richardson had walked out of the colony in 1896, protesting against 'communal' agriculture. They had wanted to convert Clousden Hill into a 'co-operative agricultural society.' Had this approach been adopted the colony would have ceased to be open to anyone who wished to join, and would have abandoned the anarchist-communist tenets of total democracy. Instead, the farm would have been restarted as a 'co-partnership', a form of co-operative promoted by some radical co-operators, but which would have had to submit its rules and annual reports to the State Registrar of Industrial and Provident Societies — anathema to any self-respecting anarchist. Membership would be limited to those who bought shares, and shareholders could include trade unions and co-operative societies outside the farm as well as those working at Clousden Hill. Walker's scheme might have overcome the colony's immediate financial weaknesses, especially the lack of capital, but it would have been at the expense of fundamental principles. Perhaps not surprisingly, the majority of the colonists rejected Walker's idea, and insisted on their 'determination... to proceed on communal lines.'[33] Walker, Miller and Richardson then left.

Robert Walker began a serious campaign to win Co-operative support for his ideas in February 1897. The first public step took the form of a letter to the *Labour Leader*, less detailed than his subsequent letter to the *Clarion*, in which he outlined a plan to take over a twenty-eight acre farm at Morpeth, to be underwritten by sales of four hundred shares at £1 each.[34] The proposal had supporters in the Jarrow and the Sunderland co-operative societies, which were substantial organisations promoting co-operative ideals. By 1894, the Sunderland society had added to its trading departments: a members' lending library of eight thousand books; a central and three-branch reading rooms, stocking twenty-six daily and thirty-six weekly newspapers together with thirty-one monthly magazines; and the Society regularly arranged lectures and classes on Co-operation. These developments were pioneered by the Society's education committee, elected by the members and chaired by an experienced educator named W.R. Rae. As a head teacher, Rae was committed to expanding education and, connecting this with his interest in Co-operative philosophy and organisation, he gradually became a major national figure in the Cooperative Movement. A similar process was under way at Jarrow where the local co-operative had also built up a popular library and lecture series. At the height of Walker's campaign to launch a co-operative agricultural society, the Jarrow co-operators held a public lecture on 'Co-operative Production' to be given by Rae who was well-placed,

through his secretaryship of an East Durham Association of co-operative societies, to facilitate Walker's access to Co-operative audiences.

Walker became a delegate to an East Durham Co-operative conference held at Boldon Miners' Hall on 3 April 1897. Its theme, 'Co-operation as Applied to Agriculture', was introduced with a paper that had been presented at the previous year's Co-operative Congress.

W.R. Rae.
Co-operative
educator.

As occasionally happens at formal meetings, nobody appeared in a hurry to say anything once the paper had been read. 'After a pause', Rae took charge by suggesting discussion of two issues: either retail societies themselves buying farms and employing labourers, or a 'self-help' model 'wherein societies and individuals might perhaps by help, advice, and purchase enable the agricultural population to help themselves.' This was an opening for Robert Walker's scheme, and the ground appears to have been carefully prepared in advance.[35]

Those delegates who spoke tended to support the principle of agricultural co-operatives, with only the CWS representative strongly concurring with 'the policy laid down in the paper', arguing that 'the stores should get the land for their own benefit... as a means of profitable investment.' He added that he 'was afraid the agricultural [labourers] would... decline to be helped' to become co-operators in their own right. At this moment, Robert Walker — 'who had been for some time a colonist at Clousden Hill Farm' — countered, stressing that 'there was a good hope of the establishment of a Northern Agricultural Co-operative Society on registered lines, and on the basis of copartnership.' Delegates from the Jarrow and nearby Boldon co-operative societies echoed Walker, and a Gateshead co-operator, although personally favouring the CWS view, disclosed that the 'Northern Sectional Board [representing all co-operative societies in Northumberland and Durham] were favourable to an attempt being made along the lines suggested by Mr. Walker, and would probably send out at an early date a circular to that effect.' The conference ended on that high note, with a Jarrow delegate inviting the East Durham co-operators to hold their next meeting at Jarrow — 'the subject to be discussed be again Agriculture, and... the delegates would come prepared to say to what extent their societies would support an... agricultural society. This was agreed.'[36]

Boldon felt like a huge success for Walker and Rae, raising the prospect that co-operators along the south of the Tyne might set-up a rival to Clousden Hill. Two months later, the issue was still being debated with 'Co-operation in Agriculture' featuring prominently on the agenda of the Northern co-operators' annual meeting. Once again, Robert Walker was present to press his case, and to cast doubts about the Clousden Hill colony ('he did not think it was paying yet').[37] But Kapper and the other colonists need not have worried. When the East Durham co-operators met at Jarrow on 3rd July it was obvious that nothing had happened since their Boldon meeting: 'delegates seemed... vaguely enthusiastic on the general principle but unable to say anything definite.' Rae was evidently disappointed, commenting later: 'our societies seemed timid and fearsome beside the question of farming' through an agricultural co-operative.[38]

What had derailed Walker's plan? He had not really understood that Co-operative leaderships and their relatively passive memberships now favoured fairly orthodox trading methods. This was only too evident when the Birtley and the Chester-le-Street co-operative societies took up farming, opting to own and administer the farms through their conventional management structures. There were still many differences between the retail co-operatives and their private trade competitors — the co-operatives had democratic rule books and attractive profit-sharing systems, for instance — but the days of pioneering new, independent co-operatives were largely over. Local societies had often become substantial social and commercial institutions, consolidating a degree of accommodation with the market economy in which they operated. Co-operators were tending to see the enlargement of their own organisations as a criterion of 'progress', rejecting in practice earlier notions of supplanting private competition with a comprehensive co-operative economy. It meant that retail societies were more likely, towards the end of the century, to open branch shops, rather than encourage the formation of new co-operatives; and they were more likely to embed bakeries and other 'productive' facilities in their own (or the CWS) trading organisations, rather than assist the launching of independent, producer societies. Robert Walker was trapped by these internal trends. In the eyes of former comrades at Clousden Hill, he had deserted the Cause, yet the 'practical' men who ran the co-operative societies saw him as just another romantic idealist. The 'Northern Agricultural Co-operative Society' never left the starting blocks.

References

1   *Armytage, op.cit.,* p. 313; *Clarion, op.cit. Northern Echo,* 11 August 1896. The full title of Michael Flurscheim's book was: *Rent, Interest and Wages or The Real Bearings of the Land Question: Private Rent the Mother of Interest, The Cause of Commercial Depressions & Social Misery,* (London, 1892). For Shaw's quotation, see Colin Spencer, *The Heretic's Feast: A History of Vegetarianism,* (London, 1993), p.279.

2   *Clarion, op.cit.*

3   L. Thompson, *op.cit.,* p.84.

4   Armytage, *op.cit.* For Snell and the London Gardens Society see Willes, *op.cit.,* p.312.

5   H. Snell, *Men, Movements and Myself,* (London, 1938 edn), pp.79, 114.

6   *Newcastle Evening Chronicle,* 27 June 1896; *Northern Echo,* 7 August 1896.

7   *Freedom,* August–September 1896.

8   *Labour Leader,* 3 August 1895.

9   *Freedom,* October 1896. See: Marie Fleming, *The Anarchist Way to Socialism: Elisee Reclus and Nineteenth-Century European Anarchism,* (London, 1979).

10 *Labour Annual, 1897,* (Manchester, 1896), p.154.

11 *The Anarchist,* (Sheffield), November 1895.

12 Home Office papers, *op.cit.*

13 *Ibid.*

[14] *Le Temps, op.cit; Northern Echo*, 11 August 1896, described Gunderson as 'a pleasant faced young fellow of about 17 or 18 years'; See Nevinson references at Chapter Four, n14 and n22; Ben Glover (Armytage, *op.cit.,* p.313); Rasmus Gunderson (b. Trondheim, Norway, 1851) is described in the 1911 Census as a tailor living in Hampshire. His death was registered at Ware, Hertfordshire, in December 1930.

[15] *Northern Echo*, 7 and 11 August 1896.

[16] *Torch, op.cit., Le Temps, op.cit.*

[17] *Torch, op.cit.*

[18] *Labour Leader*, 12 September 1896.

[19] *Co-operative News, op.cit.* See, also, note 21 below.

[20] Cited in P. Corder, *The Life of Robert Spence Watson,* (London, 1914), pp.179–180.

[21] *Co-operative News, op.cit.* The reference to Canada may suggest that the group were Russian Doukhobors, an egalitarian and pacifist religious people who suffered severe persecution under the Tsarist regime. They were helped to emigrate to a remote part of Canada by British Tolstoyans and Quakers.

[22] *Freedom*, March 1896.

[23] *Labour Leader, op.cit.*

[24] *Freedom*, October 1896.

[25] *Labour Leader, op.cit.*

[26] Cited in *Co-operative News*, 12 September 1896.

[27] *Labour Annual, op.cit.*

[28] *Labour Leader, op.cit.*

[29] *Co-operative News, op.cit.*

[30] P. Kropotkin, 'What Man can Obtain from the Land', in *Co-operative Wholesale Societies' Annual for 1897*, (Manchester, 1897), pp.358–394.

[31] *Freedom*, August 1897.

[32] *Clarion,* 20 February 1897.

[33] *Co-operative News*, 10 April 1897.

[34] *Labour Leader,* 13 February 1897.

[35] *Co-operative News, op.cit.*

[36] *Ibid.*

[37] *Co-operative News*, 5 June 1897.

[38] W.R. Rae, 'East Durham District Association Report', *Co-operative Congress Report, 1898*, (Manchester, 1898), p. 85.

A COMMUNIST COLONY.

CLOUSDEN HILL FARM.

[By Our Special Commissioner.]

Come, I will make the continent indissoluble;
I will make the most splendid race the sun ever yet
shone upon!
I will make divine magnetic lands,
            With the love of comrades,
                With the life-long love of comrades.

It is not to be supposed that the Free Communist Colony at Clousden Hill, near Forest Hall, could exist for over a year without attracting notice, favourable or otherwise.

"How did you get on with your neighbours?" I asked Comrade Kupper, who was showing me round the farm.

"At the beginning," he said with a smile, "they didn't seem to understand us. They had a strong objection to our working on Sundays, and the boys used to come shouting round the place: 'Who killed Christ?' evidently taking us for Jews. Now that people see we mean business and have come to stay there is no disrespect; quite the reverse."

All innovators, I opined, have had the same experience and some have had to spend their lives misunderstood and unsympathised with. Not so these Free Communists. One of the first to give them encouragement was Prince Kropotkin, and they asked him to act as treasurer. His reply was a characteristic one. He took so little care of his own money, he said, that he dare not be trusted with other people's accounts. When he was lecturing in Newcastle in January last he paid the colony a visit, and was highly pleased with the practical nature of the work that had been undertaken. One of the books in the colony's library, a capital work by Grassent on horticulture, was presented by him, and bears this inscription on the flyleaf:

To the comrades of the young colony with heartiest
good wishes and best sympathies.
February 6th, 1896.   P. Kropotkin.

Tom Mann was another of their visitors, who freely acknowledged that whilst others were wasting their breath in argument, these men were reducing principles to action. Canon Moore Ede came over from Gateshead to see them, and acknowledges that the actual inspection of the farm has made a deep impression on him. The Bishop of Newcastle has written to say he will pay them a visit, and they are shortly to have the company of M. Plürscheim, the author of "Rent, Interest, and Wages."

Returning now to my description of the actual work accomplished on the farm, I may mention that whilst attending to the cultivation of vegetables the colonists are not neglecting the remunerative department of fruit.

"We have bought," said Comrade Kapper, "about 2,000 fruit bushes—currants, gooseberries, &c.,—to replace the old wood that we found on the place when we took it, and which was not worth keeping. We are also starting a small orchard."

I saw that orchard: thinly dotted through with healthy trees of standard quality apples, all having taken kindly to the soil, and giving evidence of being a profitable investment. Returning to the vegetable gardens, I had explained to me as we sat down in front of a fine growth of Dr. Maclean peas, the whole art and science of the succession of beds.

"The first year you manure the bed heavily and plant it with cabbages, celery, leeks, &c.; second year, no manure: crop: potatoes, carrots, parsnips, beet, and other roots; third year, good dressing of ashes to grow peas, beans, &c.; and the fourth year, the bed is used for general purposes, nursery for young plants, &c. The only failure we have this year is wheat; the weeds have thrown it back."

One of the most profitable vegetables is peas, the beds being planted to mature a fortnight after each other, so as to have a constant supply for the market. Mr Kapper did not think much of early potatoes. Unless they were very early they were not worth bothering with. Clarke's Maincrop is the kind mostly planted at the farm. The colonists have in view the building of a long shed for a mushroom bed and for the forcing of rhubarb. There are some frames containing cucumbers, also a bed of marrows; but it is desired to erect more frames and—as I said in my first article—a second glass house as big as the one already there.

"One man can attend to two houses," said Mr Kapper, still on his pet theory of intensive culture.

Then we had a look at the animals, Nancy, their first cow, having meanwhile created a diversion by getting into the corn. There are four cows and a calf, whilst the hen-run contains 140 head of poultry.

"We found 37 birds here when we came," said Kapper; "most of them old stagers, who ought to have died long ago. We bought new stock, and now principally have Langshans for table purposes, and Leghorns for laying."

This collection also includes Plymouth Rocks, game, &c., whilst fifty ducks, mostly Pekins, bred from five old birds, waddle contentedly between the currant bushes. Last winter about fifty geese and turkeys were fed for market, and the colonists used to sit up all night plucking and dressing them. About half a dozen hutches contain rabbits, which Kapper fondled with such tenderness that I asked him how he could have the heart to kill them. The cowbyre is also shared by a many and two kids. Comrade Richardson's little girl was carrying one of these about in her arms, making a pretty picture. The animal that pays the rint was there in the shape of a fine sow, whilst further away, inhabiting a duck erce till time is afforded to build another badly-wanted pig-sty, two store piglets are passing a contented existence, punctuated with grunts. Near at hand is a beehive, presented by Mrs Punshon, who shares her husband's interest in the infant colony, but the bees are "awa' amang the blooming heather" at present, as all decent well-behaved bees ought to be. In the stable we found Paddy II., used for taking the vegetable cart to market, Paddy I. doing the heavier work on the farm. The inscription on the trap is interesting, and I give it:—

FREE COMMUNISTIC AND CO-OPERATIVE COLONY,
CLOUSDEN HILL.

Northern Echo,
11 August 1896

So far all has been utilitarian : the colonists have had their hands full of the absolutely necessary, leaving no time for ornamentation; but there is a scheme for cleaning out a pond near the house, planting it round with more willows, and laying out a flower garden close by. Indeed flowers have already been planted there, notably a fine lot of asters, but the cows found the latter very appetising, and with true utilitarian instinct cleared the lot off. Kapper bore this raid philosophically, but he grieves when the depredations extend to the vegetable beds. - "No cabbage is sweet enough for them," he exclaimed pathetically.

By the time we had made the tour of the farm it was the tea hour, and I entered the kitchen where, round a plain deal table, the colonists assemble for their meals. Breakfast is taken at 7 in the morning, dinner at 12, tea at 5, and there is a light supper of fruit or cheese, milk, &c, at 8.30, bedtime being about 9.30 or 10. Meat is partaken of three or four times a week, but otherwise the diet inclines to vegetarian, stewed fruit, preserves, and whole meal bread, entering largely into it. In a visit which I paid subsequently to the barn, "where the Anarchists make their bombs," as Kapper jokingly informed me, I found Comrade Gunderson, a pleasant-faced young fellow of 17 or 18 years, engaged in the alarming operation of grinding the corn by hand with a Sutcliffe mill, the colony consuming about ten stones a week. The visitor to this colony must not expect the same niceties that obtain under conditions of specialised labour. These people are just now hewing their way towards independence through a thorny thicket, and the ntile comes before the dulce. The latter will succeed in due course, as was expressed by Mrs Walker in answer to a question of mine as to how she liked the life. "Oh, pretty fair ; it will be much better later on."

Mrs Judge's experience was that there was plenty of work, no time for idleness. If, as Carlyle writes, "In Idleness alone there is perpetual despair," then this colony will always have Hope for a companion.

I glanced at the old-fashioned fireplace and asked Mrs Walker how the oven went. "Oh, very well, when she once gets started, but she takes a lot of firing" was the reply.

Stretched lazily before the fire was a black and white cat, which Kapper introduced to me as the animal that polished off their rats.

"And polishes off the chickens too," said Mrs Walker with emphasis. "I saw that he had one by the neck;" which undesirable propensity is duly noted by Kapper as something to be corrected.

By this time the colonists had come in from their work, and had seated themselves round the table. Taking them according to the schools of thought they represented, there were Comrades Walker, Gunderson, and Davies, Anarchists ; Comrades Walker and Richardson, advocates of State Socialism ; Comrades Brown, a Scarborough schoolmaster (he was absent on this occasion), and Bumstead, the Nottingham shoemaker, Independent Labour party men ; and Comrade Elder, a member of the Home Colonisation Association. The preparative work already accomplished on the holding has been mainly done by five men : Comrades Walker, Kapper, Dipper, Davies, and Gunderson. The others are more recent arrivals, and the last comer is Comrade Short, a man out of employment who has found a refuge here. Lively discussions these men must have in the evenings, when there is a brief respite from work, and when they gather round the fire with their pipes. Even at the tea-table an energetic but perfectly good-humoured discussion arose

between Judge (formerly an engineer), who was one of the best speakers of the Glasgow banch of Social Democrats, and Kapper, who has been connected with the Anarchist movement since 1882, as to the part the Anarchists played in the recent Congress in London. Let me here clear away a possible misconception on the subject of Anarchism. Anarchists, as Kapper explained to me, are not Terrorists : they have no sympathy with the people who throw bombs and use the assassin's knife. "I was," he admitted, "at one time as much a believer in violence as anyone ; I now see that violence is no remedy." The logic of the Anarchist position is that, with each man ruling himself, there is no need of rule. A beautiful dream ! but all the more reason for admiring the Clousden-hill men, who are trying to put it into practice.

The only member who has left the colonists is Comrade Dipper, and this not through any quarrel with his associates, but through an unfortunate dispute arising through a misconception with the landlord of a house he had rented. If a colonist dies and leaves wife or children these are the charge of the colony; if he has any wishes outside the supply of food and clothing from the common stock, he can gratify them by means of a little spending money furnished to each. Every Sunday afternoon all the adult members of the colony assemble together to pass their weekly balance-sheet and decide on future operations. There is no authority, and all that is expected from each is a fair day's work. And these men in their revolt against a condition of things which produces great masses of unemployed require no compulsion in their daily tasks. They have realised only too well the truth of Carlyle's observation : "Liberty, I am told, is a Divine thing. Liberty, when it becomes the 'Liberty to die by starvation,' is not so divine !" Side by side with these bitter words, written more than fifty years ago (ought we not to have changed since then ?) place an incident in the life of Comrade Davies. There was a great unemployed demonstration in London, and the latter, smashing a jeweller's shop window, told the clamorous crowd to help themselves. The law tolerates not such rough and ready methods of equalisation of wealth, and Davies' paid the penalty in eighteen months' imprisonment.

"I call it an act of despair," said Kapper, in relating the incident to me. "If Society breeds desperate men, it must expect desperate actions. The age is too far advanced for men to starve quietly."

(To be concluded.)

Chapter Four
Liberty, Fame, Romance

Over time, barriers between the villagers of Forest Hall and the anarchists dissolved. The comings and goings at Clousden Hill Farm may have been regarded as odd, but 'some very good friends' were made.[1] As new arrivals outgrew the Farm's large house and three small cottages, the colonists began to move into the village, renting four family-size houses by the middle of 1897. With the colony's children mixing with their local counterparts at the district's Board school,[2] it became commonplace for children from the surrounding villages to play at the Farm. One of the colonists named 'Harry Lawson... a Scotsman [who] had been in the USA as a professional golfer' taught his game to the children. Ben Glover recalled that Lawson 'was the first one I ever saw play golf and as a lad I and Stanley Bumstead used often to knock golf clubs up and down the grass field.'[3]

Local contacts did little to dilute the anarchist-communist principles that influenced daily life. When Jim Connell, author of *The Red Flag*, visited Clousden Hill in November 1897 he found that the colonists 'ate all their meals together. The diet is about that of an ordinary workman. One is a vegetarian, and the others enjoy a sufficiency of meat every day. The Colony provides clothing as it is needed, and one shilling per week is allowed to each adult for pocket money. Considering that there is only one tee-totaller and one non-smoker outside the women, this can hardly be considered excessive.'[4] Other accounts mentioned that the 'wage-system' was completely avoided, with every member working 'according to his or her ability, and enjoy[ing] equally all the Colony can grant.'[5] The anarchists of Clousden Hill remained 'essentially Anarchists' with 'few possessions' and a way of life that may have looked 'monastic' but was 'like a family.'[6]

Another feature of the colony in 1897 was that a clear division of labour between men and women was apparent. Jim Connell observed 'the women do the cooking and the mending and nothing more, whilst the washing, which is heavy, is done by the men.'[7] This was probably something of a gloss since the women had most of the responsibility for the children. And the burden of work on the women would have been considerable because they were always in the minority — as few as two women to fifteen men and four children according to Frank Kapper in August,[8] and three women to nine men and four children by November.[9] Kapper, at least, was concerned about this imbalance, and appealed in *Freedom* for 'female comrades who are accustomed to a simple life and are willing to help in our efforts... to start a comparatively free existence which may, in many respects, be preferable to capitalist slavery.'[10]

It is difficult to be exact about number of women who lived at Clousden Hill at any one time, but the *Northern Echo*'s sympathetic journalist interviewed four women in August 1896 for an article based entirely on discussions with the women 'as they were engaged in darning and mending after the weekly washing.' It seems that the women had come with their families, in part because the colony offered an alternative to their husbands' unemployment, and the choices open to working class women were severely limited. Mrs. Walker, the first woman to live at the colony, when asked how she liked the idea of communal life, replied: 'Well, there was no liking about it; need has no choice; he'd been out of work, and I came with him.' She added that 'the first few months had been a time of heavy struggle.' The women were all politically committed and kept 'themselves well informed on labour questions from the *Clarion* and labour prophet papers.' In common with all the colony's members, the women found that work meant 'too little time for intellectual development.' Stanley Bumstead's mother spoke of how she was 'sorry to miss the opportunity of hearing lectures and addresses, especially when delivered by women.' The women, she thought, 'had the power of bringing it home to you in a way that a man never could.' There was strong respect for female socialist propagandists, with regret that Carolyn Martyn had died through being worn out 'in her constant efforts for the benefit of women workers', combined with much respect for Enid Stacy ('the one for women's rights') and for Kittie Conway (Katherine Bruce Glasier) who 'has the heart to carry the men [with] her lecture on the Cry of the Children' that was regarded as 'grand.' It had been hard 'at first to being separated from their friends and from the opportunity for any outing for pleasure's sake alone.' But 'any sacrifice', as Mrs. Richardson said, was repaid 'by the entire absence of carking care and anxiety respecting the wherewithal to supply the daily board... There is no growing old and miserable over the thought of how and where the next meal is to come from.'

Insightfully, the journalist acknowledged the 'labour of the woman worker in contrast to that of the man' in a context where the work of all was 'constant' and 'continual.' This was 'fitly expressed by one of the women' who said 'that the men are better off than us women in one way — they work hard and they work long, but when they are done, they are done. A woman's always at it, no respite when she's got over the baking and the washing, and she's sided away; there's the mending and the knitting, and there's always another meal to come.' The journalist's impression was 'that the women whilst not exactly enamoured with the life, were fully prepared to labour together shoulder to shoulder for the mutual benefit of their comrades; they fully realised that all would not be clear sailing, and were ready to meet difficulties cheerfully and to take their share in surmounting them.' The women's lives were summarised as 'cooking, cleaning, washing, mending, and knitting for all members of the colony, numbering 24. They distribute the work equally, differing at times as to the best method of performing their duties, but always labouring in perfect harmony. In addition to this they prepare meals for large parties who visit the place. They have provided for as many as seventy in one day, the meal being served on large tables placed outside.' According to Mrs. Bumstead, this 'makes our work much harder, but it has a good side, it adds to the income, and we all benefit by that.' The women's day generally began about 7 am and ended 'whiles about half past ten, whiles eleven, just depends how much we have to talk about' said Mrs. Judge. All felt that the children's bed hour was 'the only time when a body gets a canny bit peace.'

Thanks to the *Northern* Echo, it's possible to know a little about the colony's children. Again, the numbers fluctuated, but in the summer of 1896 there were reported to be thirteen (together with the four women and nine men). The visiting journalist remarked on how healthy the 'fresh, chubby-looking boys and girls' seemed to be from 'roaming at will in the fresh, pure air. Their playground is far removed from the gutter or the street', and they had access to animals for play and nurture. Above all, the children were given loving care by the adults, demonstrating 'the meaning involved in the comradeship of the communistic life ... carried out in the right spirit.' To prove the point, the example of Comrade Elders was related in terms that would have pulled at Victorian heart-strings: 'A widower with four children has joined the colonists. Men and women alike welcome the motherless ones in the bond of good fellowship. In word and deed they will be dealt with as the children of those who are blessed with both parents. In such cases, it is clear that much depends upon the wise influence of the women of the colony. With her rests the greater share of the work for the early impressions that shape their future... What particularly impressed me in the attitude of the women towards the children was the uniform gentleness and kindness, and yet quiet decisiveness, with which they spoke to them.' The children benefited as well from the colony's diet that appeared to be wholesome and varied. The women provided huge meals including a 'stack of whole-meal bread... large, nutritious loaves', made with corn hand ground by the colonists, quickly demolished by 'hearty, hungry workers.' Ben Glover later recalled the bread as 'sweet as a nut.' There were four meals a day, including 'a light supper of fruit or cheese, milk &c', meat three or four times a week 'but otherwise the diet inclines to vegetarian, stewed fruit, preserves, and whole-meal bread entering largely into it.'[11]

The quest for a libertarian life-style remained primary, reinforced by occasional public declarations that 'in all personal affairs... the members have full liberty.'[12] 'We delight in liberty', Kapper was fond of saying, pledging that he would be the first to leave if there was any change.[13] Where adult relationships were concerned, some social conventions were set aside, particularly over marriage. Several colonists had married either in church or at register offices, but others lived as companions without formal marriage. There was no tangible evidence of the sexual freedom supposedly found at the Whiteway Colony, despite Henry Nevinson's belief, written twenty-six years later, that for men there was the temptation to 'choose which woman he would like to love.' Nevinson seemed to judge women by their sexual appeal, under-lined by his further claim that he only ever saw one 'attractive' woman at the colony, 'a red-haired, charming person in a pale blue dress.'[14] Overall, life at Clousden Hill was meant to be happy and Ben Glover remembered that the colonists 'used to have some very jolly social evenings. Rolf Wanderstick [Rudolph Wanderlick] with his mandolin, Charles Davis recitations and others singing a song or two. My father was a good baritone and used to sing a few songs for them.'[15]

Work on the farm was still very hard, of course, especially for those who had to get up in the small hours of the morning, put together a horse-and-cart full of produce and then drive to Newcastle market for 3 am each day. By the autumn of 1896, the men had taken on distinct responsibilities for aspects of farm work. One man spent much of his time looking after the animals ('in which he had an intense interest'), two others took care of the greenhouses and frames, and others did general outdoor jobs.[16] Sundays were equally busy because they were often set aside as 'open days' for 'affluent visitors' who came to buy produce, at a cheaper rate than shop prices,[17] with sometimes as many as '250 invading the place.'[18] The children played a part by selling flowers at dances in Newcastle.[19] Flowers were popular, with large sales of chrysanthemums, orchids (grown by a colonist from Brussels[20]), and roses were the 'speciality of the Colony which had 3,000-4,000 rose trees.'[21] Tomatoes and cucumbers were grown in the four glasshouses built by August 1897, and the colonists did all the 'joinery, glazing, mason-work and plumbing' on the farm, sometimes assisted by visiting supporters.

Henry Nevinson, describing a visit that he made in January 1897, regarded Kapper as the 'most capable man on the farm' and found 'anarchs [sic] all building a wall for new glasshouse — Kapper, young Gunderson, Shrw [sic] affectionate Davies, & Scott, perhaps name Short or Strong and a sturdy son of Sheleswig [sic] with hair all on end in hiding, probably a deserter. Kapper showed me round & talked in his rapid & helpful style, describing the great contest with the S.D.F. member [Walker?] and his present position. He still firmly believes that the farm is the starting point of a great social & industrial revolution. All was very dirty and unkempt, ill-weeded & unorganised, but there was work & hope. The leeks, cabbages... celery, strawberries, rosies, parsnips were good but wanted labour... I had tea with his home-ground bread & celery, & came away splashing threw [sic] the lanes in the dark.' Despite Nevinson's slightly disparaging impression, he returned next day to help out:

'Early on the train to Benton & the farm. Worked all day at painting the glasshouses & ...planning. Gunderson mostly with me. Dinner of pork, mashed mangowizels [sic], suet pudding & treacle. Long converse on Alexander & Strumbouleff of Bulgaria — good talk with Rolf and a Dane on way to station. Evening alone with J.L.' It's not clear who 'J.L.' was, but Nevinson then spent two days and an outing to Durham with him or her before leaving Newcastle on 9th January in 'drifting snow.'[22]

As always, there were challenges. The land at Clousden Hill was found to hold a clay layer, hindering cultivation. Finance, too, was an ever-present problem, despite a cumulative investment of 'over £1,200' since 1895, including £350 from the colonists themselves, £70–£80 from 'sympathetic outsiders', and the balance in the form of an interest-free loan from 'the treasurer, William Key.'[23] Shortage of money became more of a headache when the flow of funds from 'sympathetic outsiders' dried up at the end of 1896. The Hammersmith Socialist Society had closed down and this seems to have dispersed the only organised group of supporters in London.

Apart from a constant lack of money, the colony was racked by traumas, natural and human, throughout the first half of 1897. On the night of 21st March a 'furious gale' swept the North of England. Its effects on Clousden Hill were devastating. Two greenhouses were blown down and other damage caused 'to the extent that markets could not be met.'[24] Undaunted, the colonists set to work on repairs and 'within a month'[25] the two green-houses were rebuilt. Then there were disappointments with the livestock. Frank Starr, who joined the colony in the spring, recalled (from a subsequent and disillusioned standpoint): 'The question of livestock provided obstacles which... proved almost insuperable. The fowls would not lay, bees refused to swarm, rabbits ran away and the ducks died. One of the newly-purchased cows proved to be blind, another went mad, whilst a third died when calving. With horses matters fared no better. One fine-

looking young beast contracted a habit of bolting whenever he was yoked, a second preferred laying down to
pulling a load, and another manifested his contempt for
things communal by kicking the front out of every cart to
which he was harnessed.'[26]

The human management of the animals may have
demonstrated the limitations of farming with a combination of good intentions but an insufficiency of specialist
knowledge. Starr believed that the colonists had an
'absolute ignorance' of livestock, though others also
remarked on the lack of experience. Ben Glover made the
point that 'it was a great pity that some of the men who
came into the Colony had not ideas for horticulture as
they were a drag on the others who were expert men at
the way of running a market garden.'[27] Another colonist
maintained that most of his comrades 'had no proper
training for treating the land properly.'[28] This deficiency
brought seemingly chaotic situations, as Frank Starr
again illustrated: 'A 30-foot smoke-shaft, built by an
amateur, who disdained the use of such a simple tool as a
plumb-line, failed to maintain its tower of Pisa-like position, and came to earth.'[29]

But commitment and enthusiasm counted for something, enabling the colonists to deal with each problem.
The smoke-shaft was quickly and properly rebuilt.
Neglected parts of the land were taken into cultivation
and in the late spring 'an air of prosperity' was
apparent.[30] Better times, however, underlined the relevance of Kropotkin's warning that an appearance of
success could attract too much outside interest. Starr
recalled how the colony was shaken by a sudden rush of
new members in the summer months: 'Would-be
Communists came tumbling in from all quarters of
Europe. Two Danes and a native of Saxony; a German
woman and her daughter; a compositor and a Professor of
Literature from Belgium, both fresh from imprisonment
for political offences; a Russian, who had suffered in
many lands for his revolutionary writings; these, among

others, presented themselves for admission. Additional to this permanent increase of membership, it was no infrequent occurrence for a party of "comrades" to dump themselves down unannounced, upon the Colony, whenever they felt the need of a summer holiday.'[31]

A different colonist wrote that the summer influx meant 'before long the Colony was flooded with more members than it could maintain. Twenty-eight men, women and children, ill-supplied with capital, with only five practical men among them, were more than the place could support.'[32] Communal meals at Clousden Hill assumed a 'tower of Babel' character. The colony always had a cosmopolitan profile and, in the middle of 1897, visitors could be welcomed in either Czech, Russian, German, French, English, Dutch, Flemish, Norwegian, Polish or Danish.[33] Although the summer increase in members contributed greatly to the internationalist mix, there had been a steady rise in permanent colonists over the preceding months. Following the departure of the Tolstoyans in the summer of 1896, a new group of people arrived from London. The spread of the colony's fame — 'one of the most promising developments of the times' according to *Freedom* in October 1896 — was stimulated by articles and 'a pamphlet describing communal life at Clousden Hill.'[34] This coverage also attracted five 'young gardeners, who had thought of starting a co-operative concern in London.' At least two members of this group, Hans ('Harry') Rasmussen, a twenty-five years old Dane, and Rudolph Wanderlick, a German, 'came North in October 1896.'[35] Another Dane and a Belgian followed shortly afterwards, and the English member of the five, Frank Starr, joined them with his wife, Elizabeth, and their daughter in March 1897.[36] The five newcomers were 'as heterogeneous in their opinions as they were in nationality... each holding different political and social views.'[37]

The fresh arrivals of summer 1897 stoked discontents. Frank Kapper remained an ardent anarchist-communist, seeking to hold the colony to its original aims. On the other hand, Harry Rasmussen and probably Rudolph Wanderlick favoured converting the colony into a co-operative on the lines originally proposed by Walker and Richardson, and may have looked with interest at the debates under way in the Tyneside Co-operative Movement between January and July 1897. Frank and Elizabeth Starr had been Tolstoyans,[38] but moved towards anarchist-communism though distancing themselves from Kapper, who in the minds of 'some of those who had acted with him' was now thought to be 'ambitious.'[39] A newer arrival with equally forceful opinions was Dr. Ladislas Gumplowicz, a Pole, whom Kropotkin was to denounce as 'an ultra-individualist.'[40] The weekly general meetings were dominated by strongly argued disagreements over the direction of travel. Rasmussen, supported by Frank Starr, pressed for tighter organisation and stricter control over new admissions to membership. Kapper and other anarchists blocked this move by invoking the colony's constitution which, under Rule 32, stipulated that 'any alteration or improvement in this statement of principles can only be done by the *unanimous* consent of the members.'[41] Insisting on discussion and unanimity as the way of settling differences, Kapper warned against the division of the colony into sectional parties that would absorb everybody's energy. Instead of making the colony more exclusive, Kapper argued that there might be room on the farm for people to practise different approaches to horticulture.[42]

None of this satisfied Rasmussen and his supporters, who felt that Clousden Hill was 'finding great difficulty in keeping its head above water... despite its temporary prosperity.'[43] The result was an impasse. Frank Starr, again not altogether unbiased, complained later that 'day after day was spent in framing sets of rules... One whole evening, indeed, was devoted to discussing whether children born upon the Colony should be admitted to membership on attaining the age of seventeen. As up to that time, no infant had made its appearance, the debate seemed, to say the least of it, a little premature.' And as complete unanimity was needed to change the rules, 'the tone of the meetings can be better imagined than described.'[44] But one concession was agreed. The 'open house' policy was abandoned, and the colonists decided to more tightly regulate visiting, announcing in *Freedom* in September: 'The Agricultural Colonists at Forest Hall desire that persons intending to visit the Colony will kindly give a week's notice of their intention, in order that the secretary may have time to write to them whether there is accommodation for visitors lodging at the place or not.'[45]

The pressures on individuals within the community at Clousden Hill were intense and, coupled with the tensions reflected in the handling of applications to visit the colony, prompted Frank Kapper to take a holiday, something he must have needed after two solid years at the farm. Away from Clousden Hill, Kapper gave an interview to a correspondent of the French daily newspaper, *Le Temps*, and this was published in Paris at the end of September.[46] The front-page interview was a combination of Kapper optimism and journalist's hype, 'depicting in glowing colours, the prosperity of the Colony, and inviting recruits to hasten to this Utopia.'[47] It only made matters worse, as several colonists reacted against alleged 'inaccuracies' and a 'far too rosy' portrayal of their living conditions (not least a reported claim that the colony had a music salon).[48] Starr, Rasmussen and other members were incensed, believing the article was likely to exacerbate problems. An 'indignant letter of protest' was sent to Kapper, who answered 'by his resignation' and departure.[49]

Frank Kapper's sudden exit heralded a period of rapid change, and crisis. Firstly, the 'summer visitors' all left, and from a total of twenty-seven or twenty-eight 'the membership was speedily reduced to twelve',[50] composed of three Danes, three Germans and three English among the men, and two English and one German among the women together with four English children.[51] Outside the colony, the *Le Temps* report sparked a dramatic increase in membership applications. The article was 'translated into nearly every Socialist newspaper in Europe, and even found its way into a Monte Videau journal. The result was that applications were received from all corners of the globe: indeed nearly the whole of an Austrian village notified its intention of starting immediately for the new Atlanta.'[52] October brought 'interviewers from many of the leading newspapers' making enquiries about the colony, 'and its name became pretty widely known.'[53] The *Newcastle Daily Chronicle*, sending a 'special correspondent', stated that the colonists 'had conferred world-wide celebrity on Clousden Hill. As letters incessantly reaching the farm prove, its name is known from one end of the earth to the other.'[54]

Readers of *Reynolds Newspaper*, a popular, labour-inclined Sunday paper, were treated to some of the arguments that had raged. *Reynolds* carried a front-page interview with Frank Kapper as 'one of the founders of the successful Anarchist Colony at Clousden Hill Farm [who] has come to London to start another Colony near Rayleigh, in Essex,'[55] apparently composed of fellow tailors.[56] Kapper set out a glowing report on Clousden Hill, insisting that it was managed 'on purely Anarchist principles. There is no Governing Committee, no majority rule, all business being settled by unanimous agreement in a public meeting of the Colonists.'[57] Two weeks later, Charles Richardson re-emerged from South Shields to fire off (again, on the *Reynolds* front-page) a few criticisms of the 'Kapper Anarchist Colony.' Richardson denied that the colony was a success, claiming that it was 'in debt, and members are leaving for the towns.' He also alleged that 'the majority of the members are not Anarchists, one member frequently blocking all business.'[58] *Reynolds*, puzzled by the contradictory accounts, despatched a reporter to contact Frank Kapper for his response. After a fortnight, a further front-page piece appeared detailing Kapper's denial that the colony had been a failure, and asserting that there had been many successes. He rounded on Richardson, claiming that 'about 2 years ago there was a secession of Social-Democrats, who wanted to change the constitution of the Colony, which is drawn up in accord with the theories of Morris and Kropotkin. Since then, few have left. Most of those members have gone because they found life in the country monotonous after the excitement of City life.'[59]

As Kapper and Richardson clashed in *Reynolds*, comments on the colony were flowing freely in other newspapers. In early November, the SDF's *Justice*, always hostile to anarchism, criticised colonies for taking socialist workers out of the industrial and political struggle when they should be spending their time spreading propaganda (ironically, a point that would have met with Kropotkin's agreement). The article was a thinly disguised barb at Clousden Hill, and went on to argue that the 'inevitable' failure of socialist colonies had the effect of attaching the label of impossibility to socialism as a whole.[60] It was a familiar argument, usually rejected by anarchists and their socialist allies on the grounds that colonies at least allowed experimentation with communal principles, as well as making available 'way stations' as bases for revolutionary agitation.[61]

The reportage rattled on. One article apparently implied that the Clousden Hill colonists were 'dirty' and lived 'like pigs.'[62] A more measured assessment was published in the *Newcastle Daily Chronicle* on 16th November. The *Chronicle* believed that the colony had achieved noteworthy agricultural successes against the odds, but claimed that 'politically it has failed', demonstrating 'the disadvantages of Communism.'[63] Beyond the boundaries of the anarchist movement only Jim Connell and the *Labour Leader* gave the remaining colonists a chance to state their case on their own terms. Connell went to Clousden Hill in mid-November, taking time off from rousing Newcastle trade unionists involved in the engineering industry's national strike and lock-out. From his visit, he wrote an article for the *Labour Leader*, drawing warm thanks in a letter from Frank Starr, now the colony's secretary: 'We have been much interviewed of late, and we have suffered from the Munchausen-like reports that have appeared, so that we feel extremely grateful to Jim Connell for his courtesy in submitting *The Labour Leader* article for approval. Fraternal greetings from all the comrades.'[64]

Connell outlined the colony's trading activities, noting that after two years 'of great difficulty', life was now 'more comfortable' and the 'prospect for the future is very hopeful.' And, as something of a romantic, Jim Connell was impressed by the colony life-style: 'The Colonists insisted on my joining them at the tea table. The meal was plain but substantial. Their sleeping accommodation, consisting largely of 'Tolstoi beds', was comfortable. I noticed that they went through their tasks with energy and freedom. They worked with a will, but, unlike the wage-slaves outside, were not afraid to raise their heads, and if necessary, drop their tools on the approach of a stranger. I came away feeling how much more enjoyable and healthy is a life led among plants and flowers than the long-drawn-out agony of those who suffer in the mill or the mine. There is talk of starting other colonies, to be run on the same lines in the Midlands and the South. If these come to anything, many of us may yet enjoy the romance of rose culture and the poetry of potato planting.'[65]

References

[1]   Ben Glover cited in Armytage, *op.cit.*

[2]   *Le Temps, op.cit.*

[3]   Armytage, *op.cit.*

[4] *Labour Leader*, 20 November 1897.

[5] *Freedom, op.cit.*

[6] *Le Temps, op.cit.*

[7] *Labour Leader, op.cit.*

[8] *Freedom, op.cit.*

[9] *Labour Leader, op.cit.*

[10] *Freedom, op.cit.*

[11] *Northern Echo*, 29 August 1896; the numbers of children, men and women were given in the *Northern Echo*, 7 August 1896; dietary details were described in the *Northern Echo,* 11 August 1896; Armytage, *op.cit.*

[12] *Freedom, op.cit.*

[13] *Le Temps, op.cit.*

[14] John Field, *Working Men's Bodies: Work Camps in Britain, 1880–1940,* (Manchester, 2013), p.86; Henry W. Nevinson, *Changes and Chances, op.cit.,* p.130. Nevinson was more explicit about his views on women in his private diaries: see Henry Nevinson Papers, Bodleian Libraries, Oxford, *Diaries,* (e/610.3); he was named in Hitler's *'Black Book'* to be arrested following a Nazi invasion (see: https://www.forces-war-records.co.uk/hitlers-black-book/person/2539/henry-wodd-nevison/)

[15] Armytage, *op.cit.*

[16] *Labour Leader, op.cit.*

[17] *Le Temps, op.cit.,* Armytage, *op.cit.*

[18] *Labour Leader, op.cit.*

[19] Armytage, *op.cit.*

[20] *Le Temps, op.cit.*

[21] *Labour Leader, op.cit.*

[22] *Co-operative News*, 26 February, 1898; Nevinson, *Changes and Chances, op.cit.,* pp.129–130; see also Henry Nevinson Papers, *op.cit.*

[23] *Labour Leader, op.cit.*

[24] *Co-operative News, op.cit.*

[25] Frank Starr, 'The Story of a Communist Experiment', *Northern Weekly*, 31 May 1902.

[26] *Ibid.* Starr's article appears to have been the unacknowledged source for much of the account of Clousden Hill written by W.C. Hart, *op.cit.*

[27] Armytage, *op.cit.*

[28] *Co-operative News, op.cit.*

[29] *Northern Weekly, op.cit.*

[30] *Ibid.*

[31] *Ibid.* Whiteway Colony experienced problems with summer visitors: Shaw, *op.cit.*

[32] *Co-operative News*, 19 April 1902.

[33] 'Communism at Clousden: The Story of an Economic and Agricultural Experiment, by a Special Correspondent' in *Newcastle Daily Chronicle*, 16 November 1897.

[34] *Northern Weekly, op.cit.* The reference to a pamphlet is intriguing. Arthur Baker intended publishing a pamphlet on the Clousden Hill Colony in his New Moral World Series of pamphlets on communist communities, but there is no evidence that this ever happened.

[35] *Newcastle Daily Journal*, 18 April 1902; Rasmussen's age may be found from the 1901 Census.

[36] *Northern Weekly, op.cit.*

[37] *Co-operative News, op.cit.*

[38] *Northern Weekly, op.cit.*

[39] *Newcastle Daily Chronicle, op.cit.*

[40] John Quail, *The Slow Burning Fuse: The Lost History of the British Anarchists,* (London, 1978), p.212. Ben Glover recalled Gumplowicz as 'Doctor Complevitz'; Armytage, *op.cit.,* p.312. Ladislaus Gumplowicz (1869–1942), was a Polish Jewish doctor and writer with strong anti-marriage opinions. He distanced himself from anarchism after the 1890s and was active in Polish and German socialist movements, and became an academic geographer. His father, Ludwig Gumplowicz, was a founder of European sociology. Ladislaus died of a heart attack in Warsaw in 1942 involved in the socialist resistance to the Nazis, teaching current affairs to the Polish underground and translating anti-Nazi publicity materials into German.

[41] *Torch, op.cit.*

[42] *Le Temps, op.cit.*

[43] *Northern Weekly, op.cit.*

[44] *Ibid.*

[45] *Freedom*, September 1897.

[46] *Le Temps, op.cit.*

[47] *Northern Weekly, op.cit.*

[48] *Newcastle Daily Chronicle, op.cit.*

[49] *Northern Weekly, op.cit.*

[50] *Ibid.*

[51] *Labour Leader, op.cit.*

[52] *Northern Weekly, op.cit.* See also *Le Temps Nouveaux*, No. 30, 20 November 1897 and the *San Francisco Chronicle,* 30 January 1898.

[53] *Co-operative News, op.cit.*

[54] *Newcastle Daily Chronicle, op.cit.*

[55] *Reynolds Newspaper*, 17 October 1897.

[56] *Newcastle Daily Chronicle, op.cit.*

[57] *Reynolds, op.cit.*

[58] *Ibid.,* 31 October 1897.

[59] *Ibid.,* 14 November 1897.

[60] *Justice,* 6 November 1897.

[61] Arthur Baker, in his pamphlet *A Plea for Communism*, (London, 1896), p.21, used Starnthwaite as an example of a colony that served as a 'red base': 'In the early days of the Starnthwaite experiment... the Colonists were engaged in communal work all the week, but on Sundays were scattered all over the Labour Churches, and ILP and SDF branches in Lancashire and Yorkshire preaching the gospel of the world's brotherhood with the more force and effect, because they were to some extent practising the life of brotherhood themselves.'

[62] Cited in *Newcastle Daily Chronicle, op.cit.*

[63] *Ibid.*

[64] *Labour Leader, op.cit.*

[65] *Ibid.* Connell also visited Whiteway, and suggested that the colonists should deal with a difficult neighbour by poisoning his cows (Shaw, *op.cit.,* p.118). The idea was not taken up!

A COMMUNIST COLONY.

WOMEN AS FARM COLONISTS
[By M. D. M.]

                                                    Deep, indeed
Their debt of thanks to her who first had dared
To leap the rotten pales of prejudice,
Disyoke their necks from custom, and assert
None lordlier than themselves but that which made
Woman and man.
          *   *   *   *   *
                                                    Everywhere
Two heads in counsil, two beside the hearth,
Two in the tangled business of the world,
Two in the liberal offices of life.

Just as constant labour is the present indispensable condition of the men on the Clousden Hill farm colony, so does continual industry represent the daily life of the four women who have decided to throw in their lot and share in a scheme which so far ensures to them the production of the necessaries of life. Only one difference—a difference which has always marked somewhat unevenly the labour of the woman worker in contrast to that of the man, and which was fitly expressed by one of the women to me—is "that the men are a bit better off than us women in one way—they work hard and they work long, but when they're done, they are done. A woman's always at it, no respite when she's got over the baking and the washing, and she's aided away; there's the mending and the knitting, and there's always another meal to come." The day I visited the colony was one of the least busy days for the women. They certainly worked uninterruptedly, but as they were engaged in darning and mending after the weekly washing I was enabled in the course of conversation to note many perhaps trivial facts, but which taken in the aggregate form important elements in the home life of the members of the colony.

The impression I gathered was that the women whilst at present not exactly enamoured with the life, were fully prepared to labour together shoulder to shoulder for the mutual benefit of their comrades; they fully realised that all would not be clear sailing, and were ready to meet difficulties cheerfully and to take their share in surmounting them. Mrs Walker was the first woman who took up her abode at the colony. In answer to my question as to how she liked the idea she said : "Well, there was no liking about it; need has no choice; he'd been out of work, and I came with him." As time passed on three women joined Mrs Walker, each in turn feeling the lack of choice and the advisability of sharing the lot of her partner. Mrs Walker described the first few months as being a time of heavy struggle. Things have vastly improved since, and as the colony prospers the women will be provided with the means of carrying on all branches of domestic work under the most improved system. Some time must necessarily elapse before this can be accomplished. Patience I should say is not the least of the virtues these women possess. The erection within the last fortnight of a new stove, which burns less fuel and cooks with less labour, gives evidence that the needs of the women will be considered. The necessity of an oven capable of saving labour and fuel was shown by a view of the stack of whole-meal bread that I saw cooked during my visit, and that in such-like and sometimes in larger quantities is cooked four times a week. "We do plenty of praying to this oven," remarked Mrs Richardson, as down on her knees she went to lift the large, nutritious loaves from their last process before being ready for consumption. A sight of how the bread disappeared was afforded a little later on, when round the tables gathered the hearty, hungry workers, who quickly demolished piles of this excellent food.

The labour of the women consists in cooking, cleaning, washing, making, mending, and knitting for all the members of the colony, numbering 24. They distribute the work equally, differing at times as to the best method of performing their duties, but always labouring in perfect harmony. In addition to this they prepare meals for large parties who visit the place. They have provided for as many as seventy in one day, the meal being served on large tables placed outside. "This makes our work much harder," said Mrs Bumstead, "but it has its good side, it adds to the income, and we all benefit by that," They rise about seven in the morning and retire "whiles half-past ten, whiles eleven, just depends how much we have to talk about," said Mrs Judge. Like all women who have the toil and care of the children themselves, they hail the youngsters' bed-hour as "the only time when a body gets a canny bit peace."

Speaking of the social and other pleasures that they most miss in the quiet and comparative isolation of the colony life, they generally agreed that they took badly at first to being separated from their friends and from the opportunity of any outing for pleasure's sake alone. Any sacrifice in this direction is repaid, as Mrs Richardson sensibly remarked, by the entire absence of carking care and anxiety respecting the wherewithal to supply the daily board. Whatever may be the result of the future of the colony the present has its bright and cheerful aspect. However hard the women may toil they have the satisfaction of knowing that the material is there to meet the demand. There is no growing old and miserable over the thought of how and where the next meal is to come from. The food is not luxurious, but it is wholesome and nutritious. Work is the only taskmaster, and the workers — men and women alike — equally share the produce of their labour. The women have sadly too little time for intellectual development, owing to the interminable making, mending, and darning which they are compelled to do, but they manage to keep themselves well informed on labour questions from the

Clarion and labour prophet papers. Mrs Bumstead was sorry to miss the opportunity of hearing lectures and addresses, especially when delivered by women. The women, she thought, had the "power of bringing it home to you in a way that a man never could."

They all spoke regretfully of the late Miss Carrie Martyn, who without doubt hastened her journey in her constant efforts for the benefit of the women workers. "Enid's the one for women's rights" (Enid Stacey), said Mrs Bumstead, "but Kittie Conway (Mrs Bruce Glasier) has the heart to carry the men. Her lecture on the 'Cry of the Children' is grand."

The children of the colony, "the ones to whom we look to for the future," as Mr Kapper remarked, kindly patting a sturdy young lad of twelve upon the head, are bright and healthy looking; the boy of twelve already frames successfully for a man's work; the younger ones enjoy the greatest boon that children can, the freedom of roaming at will in the fresh, pure air. Their playground is far removed from the gutter or the street, and there is little fear of the fresh, chubby-looking boys and girls that I saw exclaiming, as a little town lad did on one of his rare visits to the country, "Bah! How big the sky grows here!" An instance which significantly shows the meaning involved in the comradeship of communistic life, if carried out in the right spirit, is proved by the following: — A widower with four children has joined the colonists. Men and women alike welcome the motherless ones in the bond of good fellowship. In word and deed they will be dealt with as the children of those who are blessed with both parents. In such cases it is clear that much depends upon the wise influence of the women of the colony. With her rests the greater share of the work for the young ones, and the responsibility of directing the early impressions that shape their future in the right course. What particularly impressed me in the attitude of the women towards the children was the uniform gentleness and kindness, and yet quiet decisiveness, with which they spoke to them. The women regard the coming winter as a time of hard work and possible hardships. They have the heart and the determination to do their best, buoyed up, I gathered, by a hope of less toiling in the future. They express entire satisfaction with the progress hitherto made, and will appreciate greater boons as they

[THE END.]

Northern Echo,
29 August 1896

Chapter Five
'And Thus Set the Sun'

'Comrades, prove your existence by your presence' pleaded an appeal placed in the *Labour Leader* by the Newcastle ILP in November 1898.[1] It was the latest of several attempts to convene a general meeting of the city's ILPers to discuss the adoption of a parliamentary candidate. But all their efforts had met with a poor response, and it seemed that the Newcastle comrades were 'taking a nap.'[2] Both socialism and anarchism were at a low ebb compared with the heady days of 1893–1897. Demoralisation had set in following the shattering defeat of the engineers' national strike in early 1898, and the relentless rise of aggressive imperialist rivalry, together with the self-image of the British people that it projected, began to reshape attitudes. Not only socialists and anarchists but even Radical Liberals found themselves shunted into the margins.

Meanwhile, friends of the Clousden Hill colony took on other preoccupations — Mrs. Dryhurst devoted more time to helping Spanish anarchist refugees — or, as with Harry Snell, they were simply exhausted: 'It was work that required more strength than I possessed, and the end came while I was speaking in the district of Newcastle-on-Tyne. For several nights I tried to give the lectures seated, but on the 5th of November 1898, the doctor whom I consulted insisted on the remaining engagements being cancelled, and I returned home with a nervous exhaustion which lasted for several years.'[3] Most of the anarchist journals had collapsed by the end of 1897. Only *Freedom* survived as a national publication although it, too, struggled with production, distribution and finance from 1898 onwards. The fate of the anarchist press indicated the general disintegration of anarchism in Britain, leaving the advocacy of communist colonies to a few activists like Billy McQueen, a Leeds anarchist. Publishing a magazine called the *Free Commune*, promoting the creation of colonies as a 'revolutionary deed', McQueen helped to keep together those anarchist communitarians active in the North of England. In June 1898 he still regarded Clousden Hill as an important part of the colony movement, presenting it as an example of how to organise a communist community — adjacent to a large town, using 'glass culture' and trading with co-operative societies.[4]

After the 'departure from pure Anarchism'[5] and the related traumas of the second half of 1897, the Clousden Hill Free Communist and Co-operative Colony was grappling with definition. The break with 'the irreconcilables'[6] was followed by a period of 'retrenchment and reform.'[7] A decision was taken to sell the 'generally unprofitable' livestock and focus on 'more intensive agriculture.'[8] Seeing the future largely in terms of plants and vegetables, the colonists built an additional glasshouse and 'preparations were made for further developments in the spring' of 1898. And 'as there were 3 gardeners and a farmer remaining, there seemed to be some possibility of success attending the new enterprise.'[9] Against this background, a renewed bid was launched to win the co-operative societies' support. Harry Rasmussen spearheaded the conversation, and found that the door remained almost half open. A boycott of Scottish co-operatives by private traders, and the not very successful performance of farms controlled directly by retail co-operatives, encouraged co-operators on Tyneside to give serious thought to their relationship with the Clousden Hill colony. Consequently, Co-operative delegates attending their Northern Sectional Conference in February 1898 arranged to see Clousden Hill farm at first hand. The visit sparked a good deal of excitement among the leaders of the local co-operatives with the Board of the Newcastle co-operative society resolving: 'That as many Directors as can make it convenient to be present attend the conference, that the Members appointed to attend meetings of the Co-operative Wholesale Society be also invited to be present, and that the Farm Manager and Gardener be requested to attend.'[10]

The visit to Clousden Hill generated a full-page report in the *Co-operative News*, recounting that 'a large number of northern co-operators paid a visit to the renowned communistic and co-operative colony.' It was a bleak and cold day when the co-operators arrived at Forest Hall in open carriages, but 'as the inspection of the Colony proceeded, interest increased.' Everyone was 'impressed with the intelligence and faith of the members of the communistic settlement', none of whom 'were amongst its original founders.' The visitors were told that the colony had been 'seriously hampered for want of capital', and that the colonists were 'anxious to cultivate a closer relationship' with the Co-operative Movement with whom they shared 'common conceptions of industrial organisation.' It was pointed out that 'the Sunderland Society in particular had been a good customer at Clousden Hill, and if the societies represented... would accept the advice... of Sunderland friends, and purchase the high-classed products of the Colony, the benefit would be a mutual one.' The colonists considered 'themselves now sufficiently equipped to supply the co-operative market on very favourable terms... [and]... they expressed themselves in terms of delight at the comparative cheapness of fuel hereat obtainable for heating the glasshouses — a considerable advantage over Southern competitors!' The *News* concluded with a generous tribute: 'What sacrifices they have made — how patiently they have endured! Obstacles innumerable have been surmounted.'[11] Rasmussen had managed to impress the potential customers.

'On returning to Newcastle the representatives of northern co-operation marched to the boardroom of the CWS in Waterloo Street,' where they held a conference on

'Co-operators and the thorough cultivation of the land.' The theme was introduced by Henry Vivian, a leading advocate of co-operative co-partnership, who praised the 'evidence of energy and skill seen at Clousden Hill.' Among those contributing to the discussion was Harry Rasmussen who told the delegates of the success of co-operative farming in 'his own country of Denmark.'[12] Rasmussen worked hard to convince the co-operators that the Clousden Hill colony now shared their view of Co-operation. So much so, that he used the visit to the farm to put distance between himself and 'the Anarchial ideas of the founders' of the colony. He criticised Kapper and the original aims as 'too extreme', claiming that 'codes of law and order were shunned, every member of the settlement was to feel free from all authority, save the promptings of conscience.' That course had proved unworkable and 'the management had been left to... a more practical set of enthusiasts.' According to Rasmussen, he and his fellow gardeners had only offered to join the colony 'provided the then members would agree to conduct matters in accord with their ideas.' The colony now had 'a defined set of rules' and was seeking registration 'as a Co-operative Productive Association',[13] a point later borne out by Frank Starr who recalled a resolution having been passed to 'transform the Communist experimental station into a horticultural co-operative society.'[14]

Clousden Hill's connections with anarchism were evaporating, but had not entirely vanished. Frank Starr insisted that the colony was 'still run upon Communist lines' during the spring and summer of 1898. The Starrs were now cast in the role of defenders of communist methods against the managerialism of Rasmussen and Wanderlick. The 'new Co-operators', wrote Frank Starr, 'retained enough of the old communal spirit to be indifferent to the allotment of profits [but] their tolerance did not extend to the question of leadership.'[15] The much reduced community was engulfed in 'quarrels about leadership',[16] and with 'but six voters' among the members 'there were two parties.'[17] Attempts to compromise proved futile, and 'the inevitable came in the departure of one Dane and the whole of the English contingent.'[18] The end of Clousden Hill as a communist colony came on 19th September 1898 with the farm 'being taken over as a private concern' by Rasmussen and Wanderlick.[19] A reference in the *Labour Annual* recorded the colony as abandoned 'owing to internal dissension.'[20] As Frank Starr concluded: 'And thus set the sun of Communism over Clousden Hill.'[21]

Well, not quite. The 'final separation' was by no means the end, simply the beginning of new phases. The Starrs and a Danish colonist, Gerry Noëlle, were paid £429 by their former comrades to relinquish their claims to Clousden Hill Farm.[22] They then moved across the Tyne to Whickham, west of Gateshead, where they founded a new 'commune' on the Whaggs Lodge Estate. This was an area that had been taken over by the Northern Allotments Society, formed in 1890 to provide land and educational assistance for 'working men' interested in becoming horticultural small-holders. The Society bought the Whaggs Lodge Estate in 1892, and increased the resident population rapidly from ten to over one hundred people.[23] For some reason, Frank Starr completely ignored the 'Whaggs Commune', on which he spent more than three years of his life, when he came to write about his Clousden Hill experiences in 1902. By then he was a deeply disillusioned man, highly critical of anarchists and communal projects: 'Angels might have lived the life, flesh and blood could not. Men and women, with all their human failings, are still too distant from the time when the lion shall lie down with the lamb.'[24]

On leaving Clousden Hill in September 1898, the Starrs were still keen on a communist life. It was left to Elizabeth Starr to write about the Whaggs Commune in letters to a relative in London. Although only fragments of her letters have survived, these reveal that the Starrs and Noëlle 'had a market garden and grew cucumbers and tomatoes.'[25] The commune gained a contract from Whickham Urban District Council to remove waste from local 'netties' for use as manure'[26] but it was all strenuous work that came to an end when Elizabeth Starr died in September 1901. She was buried in St. Mary's Church-yard, Whickham, and a financially broken Frank Starr finally returned to London with his daughter in 1905.[27]

Back at Clousden Hill, the former anarchist colony had not necessarily changed into a 'private concern.' Under the control of Rasmussen and Wanderlick, the farm had become the 'Clousden Hill Co-operative Nurseries Co. Ltd.' The 'co-operative' took over debts accumulated by the colony amounting to about £1,500. Rasmussen had 'secured from relatives' some money to invest, but the two partners 'were harassed for cash from the very begin-ning.' The outcome of the February visit by the

Clousden Hill Farm in 1979
PHOTO: GORDON GASKIN

co-operators had turned out to be disappointing, with no increase in sales to co-operative stores. Simultaneously, market gardening was being taken up by private competitors, and in fact a family firm of nurserymen and florists had moved from Gateshead to the Clousden Hill House Farm, adjacent to the colony, in 1897. A concerted attempt to expand the sales of flowers failed when the South African War depressed the market 'and the flowers would not sell' with disastrous consequences for Rasmussen and Wanderlick.[28] The two men seem to have quarrelled around this time, and Wanderlick left.[29]

Eventually, the Clousden Hill Co-operative Nurseries went bankrupt, but not before Rasmussen had sold the greenhouses to outflank any financial claims by the landlord, Mr. Punshon. In April 1902, the farm's affairs were examined at the Newcastle Bankruptcy Court, where there was a large area of vagueness about the financial history of the enterprise. Rasmussen told the Court that £70 was owed to a Mr. Crawford Smith (possibly for seeds) and that William Key 'had formerly financed the Colony and had the lease. £500 was due to him.' This really was the end, apart from highly critical obituaries written by a few ex-colonists. On the other hand, the *Newcastle Daily Chronicle* offered the kind consolation that the colony had not entirely failed as 'astonishing results' had been won from the land.[30]

The men and women who had searched for a 'free communist' society at Clousden Hill, arousing international attention, faded into largely unrecorded history and only glimpses of them remain. Frank Kapper continued his association with colonies in Essex, where even in the 1980s his name was still familiar to very aged one-time local colonists.[31] Harry Rasmussen emigrated to the United States after the bankruptcy. He kept in touch with old friends at Forest Hall, and Ben Glover's sister visited him when he was fairly elderly.[32] Rasmussen died at Santa Monica, and by a coincidence Rudolph Wanderlick died further up the American West Coast at

Ben Glover *(FAR RIGHT IN DARK SUIT)* with his sister,
Mrs Cheetham, and her husband who visited
Harry Rasmussen in California
PHOTO: MRS MARJORIE GRAY

Seattle. Wanderlick had also emigrated after the death of his wife whom he had met at Forest Hall.[33] Frank Starr went back to London, perhaps taking up his old trade as a printer. But he did write a lengthy account of his involvement at Clousden Hill, stimulated to do so by the 1902 bankruptcy. It was published in Teddy Ashton's *Northern Weekly*, produced by the Bolton socialist Allen Clarke. And to earn some much-needed money, Starr wrote at least one short story — a tale of poverty and good luck — for the *Northern Weekly*. After 1902, Allen Clarke worked to create a form of Tolstoyan-anarchist land colony at Daisy Hill, Poulton-le-Fylde, near Blackpool, and ironically a degree of the inspiration may have came from contact with Starr.[34] Then there was William Key, without whom the story would not have been possible at all. As a tolerant benefactor, Key must have carried most of the costs of the Clousden Hill colony. Not a man to be distracted by the occasional set-back, he could be found in 1911 throwing himself into Tom Mann's movement for industrial syndicalism and 'workers power.'[35] Of the others who gave a year or two of their lives to the Cause of 'free communism', we know very little.

References

[1] *Labour Leader*, 12 November 1898.

[2] *Ibid.*

[3] Snell, *op.cit.*, pp.124–125.

[4] *The Free Commune*, June 1898.

[5] *Northern Weekly, op.cit.*

[6] *Co-operative News, op.cit.*

[7] *Northern Weekly, op.cit.*

[8] *Labour Leader*, 20 November 1897.

[9] *Northern Weekly, op.cit.*

[10] Newcastle upon Tyne Co-operative Society Ltd., Minutes of the Board of Directors, 8 February 1898.

[11] *Co-operative News*, 26 February 1898.

[12] *Ibid.*

[13] *Ibid.*

[14] *Northern Weekly, op.cit.*

[15] *Ibid.*

[16] *Co-operative News,* 19 April 1902.

[17] *Northern Weekly, op.cit.*

[18] *Ibid.*

[19] *Co-operative News, op.cit.*

[20] *Labour Annual*, 1899, (Manchester, 1898), p.115.

[21] *Northern Weekly, op.cit.*

[22] *Newcastle Daily Journal, op.cit.*

[23] Joseph W. Wakinshaw, 'The Northern Allotment Society' in *Journal of the Board of Agriculture*, July, 1905, pp.202–209.

[24] *Northern Weekly, op.cit.*

[25] Gateshead Central Library, Local Studies Collection.

[26] Information supplied by the late Tom Marshall, former Gateshead Local Studies Librarian.

[27] Tom Marshall and Gordon Gaskin.

[28] *Newcastle Daily Journal, op.cit.*

[29] Armytage, *op.cit.,* p.314.

[30] *Newcastle Daily Chronicle*, 18 April 1902.

[31] Information supplied by Ken Weller who was familiar with several former Essex colonists.

[32] Information supplied by the late Jean Gleghorn, a local historian in the Forest Hall area who tried for years to convince her neighbours that there really was an anarchist colony in the village!

[33] Armytage, *op.cit.*

[34] See: Paul Salveson, 'When Socialism was Popular' in *The Chartist*, June-August 1984; 'Getting Back to the Land: The Daisy Colony Experiment' in *Labour's Turning Point in the North-West 1880–1914*, North West Labour History Society (1984), pp.31-36; *Lancashire's Romantic Radical: The Life and Writings of Allen Clarke/Teddy Ashton,* (Huddersfield, 2009), pp.46–48. Also Bellamy and Saville, *op.cit.,* (1979), vol. 5., pp.64–70.

[35] G. Brown (ed), *The Industrial Syndicalist,* (Nottingham, 1974 reprint), p.205.

Chapter Six
Endnote

The history of the Clousden Hill Free Communist and Co-operative Colony is fascinating in its own right. But those who built the colony were not isolated eccentrics. They were part of a diffuse movement of land colonisers that continued for years after the decline of Clousden Hill. This was as true on Tyneside as elsewhere. In January 1901, for instance, a T. Downing of Gateshead announced that he was 'acquainted with several men who are now trying to form an experimental colony' as an 'opening for a great reform in some of the conditions under which we are at present compelled to live.'[1] Had Downing succeeded — there were obstacles in finding suitable land and raising funds — then, arguably, there would have been three land colonies on Tyneside at the same time.

Nor did the fate of the Clousden Hill colonists entirely blunt anarchism along the Tyne. Eclipsed for a few years, anarchists had reappeared by 1907 when there were signs of activity again in Newcastle and Sunderland.[2] An anarchist club was functioning at Newcastle in 1909, and by 1912 it had been joined by 'a very active Anarchist group' in the pit village of Chopwell, just south of Gateshead. The Chopwell anarchists, helped financially by George Davidson (who had made a fortune out of selling Kodak cameras) opened their own club in a former shop: 'The Anarchist meeting place became known as the "Communist Club" in the village... an established... centre of left-wing political activity.'[3] Much of the anarchism in Chopwell was orchestrated by a Workers' Freedom Group that included Will Lawther, who much later was to become a leader of the miners' union, a pillar of the Labour Party hierarchy and a knight of the realm.

Before the First World War, and directly afterwards during Chopwell's 'Little Moscow' period, Lawther was a dedicated revolutionary, expressing his politics initially through anarchism. In that connection, he participated in an anarchist national conference, held at the British Socialist Party club in Newcastle's Leazes Park Road, over Easter 1914. The conference took place in private with the *Newcastle Daily Chronicle* reporter who was turned away at the door remarking that the anarchists did not look like desperate revolutionaries: 'had you not been told who they were you might have regarded them as members of a young men's mutual improvement society... extremists of an inoffensive kind.'[4]

Lawther made no secret of his 'advanced' views, as he demonstrated at a public meeting called to explain anarchism in the Co-operative Hall, Darn Crook, Newcastle, towards the close of the 1914 conference: 'In spite of all the pleadings and warnings of the so-called official section of the labour movement, with which Anarchy was solely concerned, there had been a revolt of the workers in the last four years. As Anarchists [we] regard this as an upheaval for the purpose of throwing over the leaders. Anarchists believed that any movement which aimed at freeing the workers must carry out its propaganda, not in the doss house of Westminster, but at work and where the work was.'[5]

This short book aimed to bring the Clousden Hill colonists to public attention again after a long period of neglect. Of course, the colony could never have survived on its own terms without an overall alteration of the economy and society. Frank Kapper, apparently, understood and accepted that reality but felt that the effort still mattered. And there is no doubt that the existence of the colony served a number of positive purposes. It offered a safe haven for victims of political persecution from all over Europe, and the value of that should not be underestimated. It helped to shape the early ILP's notions of a socialist economy and community. It introduced the Co-operative Movement to one of its periodic examinations of fundamental principles. It provided a focus for an anarchist movement elaborating libertarian ideas in a largely hostile environment. And it gave a few people a chance to taste a different kind of life. All in all, not a bad balance sheet.

References

[1] *Co-operative News,* 19 January 1901.

[2] Quail, *op.cit.,* pp.250, 253, 278–279.

[3] Les Turnbull (ed), *Chopwell's Story,* (Gateshead, 1978), np. Quail, *op.cit.,* pp.278–279, records that Lawther and his friends established a Workers' Freedom Group, which was part of a federation of groups fighting for an anarchist-communist form of society. Lawther also moved freely through the various organisations of the Left before the First World War, apparently seeing no rigid distinctions between them at local level. See: Bellamy and Saville, *op.cit.,* (1984), vol. 7., pp.140–144.

[4] *Newcastle Daily Chronicle,* 14 April 1914.

[5] *Ibid.* 13 April 1914. See, too, Lewis H. Mates, 'The Syndicalist Challenge in the Durham Coalfield before 1914' in Alex Pritchard, et.al (eds), *Libertarian Socialism: Politics in Black and Red,* (Basingstoke, 2012).

Also available from Five Leaves

Left for the Rising Sun, Right for Swan Hunter
The Plebs League in the North East of England 1908-1926
by Robert Turnbull
81 pages, 978-1-910170-07-6, £6.99

Riot: South Shields 1930 — Britain's First Race Riot
A playscript by Peter Mortimer
In English and Yemeni Arabic
120 pages, 978-1905512-49-2, £6.99

The Last of the Hunters
Life with the Fishermen of North Shields
by Peter Mortimer
131 pages, 978-1-905512-21-8, £6.99

Available from bookshops or, post free,
from Five Leaves
www.fiveleaves.co.uk
www.fiveleavesbookshop.co.uk